# The College Project

By Tyler Hensley

# Table of Contents

## PART I

### THE VALUE OF COLLEGE

# PART II

## DEEPER DIVES

For those who think they can't afford it.

Special thanks to Krista Meyers for her feedback, encouragement, and brainstorming support in this updated edition.

# PART I

# THE VALUE OF COLLEGE

---

"A cynic knows the price of everything, and the value of nothing." - Oscar Wilde

# 1

# It's Your Decision

1. Think of yourself as a "successful" adult. What does your life look like?

_____

_____

_____

2. What interests you? What do you want to get better at? Could this knowledge or skill be useful in a career, or do you see it more as a hobby?

_____

_____

_____

_____

3. Do you see college as part of your future? Why or why not?

_____

_____

_____

_____

*Everything you've done in your twelve years of schooling comes down to this.*
*- Sophie P.*

As high school ends, it's time to think about how you'd like to spend your days as a working adult. How do *you* measure success? Do you want to help others? Make "a lot" of money? Spend all day outdoors? Have flexibility to spend quality time with your kids as they grow up? Enjoy going to work most days, even Mondays?

Thought Box:

The College Project is mainly about supporting you in choosing a path after high school. Many students find success in adulthood without a college degree, and if that's the path you *want* to take, that's great.

But if you're choosing that path because you feel like you *can't* afford college, we need you to know that many assumptions about college costs aren't accurate – much has changed in recent decades – some for worse, and some for better.

Many students choose the "cheapest" pathway after high school without looking at the long-term costs and benefits of **all their options**. So that's what we're going to walk through in this book – an investigation into the real costs and benefits of your options for college. Simply put, we don't want you to skip out on college based on the idea that you can't afford it.

You can be an influencer, web developer, auto mechanic, certified underwater welder, chef, or correctional officer without a college degree. You can also enlist in the military and, after 36 months on active duty, use the G.I. Bill to help pay for college if you decide it's important to you.[1]

However, many people without a college degree have faced an uphill battle in the last decade. Since the recession in 2008, there are 5.5 million *fewer* jobs for those with a high school diploma or less, and there are 8.6 million *more* jobs for those with a bachelor's degree or higher.[2]

Given the number of job opportunities, most students will greatly benefit from earning a bachelor's (4-year) or associate's (2-year) degree. **Even if you DON'T KNOW what you want to do**, a college degree will give you the flexibility to change careers if you need *or* want to.

With access to a greater variety of jobs, you might even LOVE your job! Who wants to continue a routine where you obsess over the day of the week ("Ahh... it's only Tuesday!") and constantly check the clock at work ("I've been here for five hours. Only three more to go!").

Sounds a little like high school, huh?

With a college degree, you can still wake up dreading work if that's the path you choose, but at least you'll get paid more for your time. It'll be your choice! The point is that college graduates typically have *more work opportunities*.

In future chapters, we'll look at the average income levels of graduates of specific universities and different career paths, but first, let's look at the ability to find work (unemployment rate) and typical income (median earnings) for people with different levels of education by education level across the United States.

---

[1] https://www.military.com/education/gi-bill/learn-to-use-your-gi-bill.html
[2] https://cew.georgetown.edu/cew-reports/americas-divided-recovery/

Table 1.1 shows the unemployment rates and median (average) weekly earnings of people 25 years old and over.

| Education attained | Unemployment rate in 2023 | Median weekly earnings in 2023 |
|---|---|---|
| High school diploma | 3.9% | $899 |
| Some college, no degree | 3.3% | $992 |
| Associate's degree | 2.7% | $1,058 |
| Bachelor's degree | 2.2% | $1,493 |
| Master's degree | 2.0% | $1,737 |

Table 1.1. Data are for persons age 25 and over. Earnings are for full-time wage and salary workers. Source: Current Population Survey, U.S. Department of Labor, U.S. Bureau of Labor Statistics. https://www.bls.gov/career outlook/2018/data-on-display/education-pays.htm

Thought Box:

First, notice the difference in unemployment rates. The higher the unemployment rate, the harder it is to find a job. As you can see:

Less Education = Higher Unemployment Rate

The table also shows that people with bachelor's degrees earn an average of **$594 more per week** than those who don't move on after high school.

 $594 extra per week might sound like a lot of money (or not), but it's $2,376 more per month and nearly $31,000 per year. If you're thinking about working for 30 - 40 years, it adds up!

## I JUST CAN'T DO FOUR MORE YEARS OF SCHOOL

You may think college will just be a harder version of high school, where you regularly ask, "When will I ever use this?" Here are a few points in response to this age-old question:

- Generally, high school is *not* about teaching you how to do your future job. (That's called "job training," and you'll do it the first few weeks of any job.) High school is about teaching you to problem solve, think critically, reason with evidence, work in diverse teams, and share ideas from the past and for the future.

- In college, you get more time and opportunity to learn about yourself and your community, build relationships with others from around the world, and make connections that can last a lifetime.

- For you to receive the greatest benefits in school, both you and your teacher(s) must invest time and effort.

So, set realistic expectations — not every college class will teach you something useful or exciting. But don't expect your college life to be so similar to your high school life. College is a place of unique benefits and great freedom. Here are a few ways college life differs from high school:

- You might have classes from 9 – 11 a.m. and then from 2 – 4 p.m., and then you're done for the day. It's not uncommon for college juniors and seniors to have no Friday classes.

  Translation: a three-day weekend. *Every weekend.* Or, for the student who registered with the schedule on the following page, a FOUR-DAY weekend every weekend. (She worked as an aide in my classroom T/Th/F.)

10

What are your thoughts on one college junior's *real* class schedule in the image below?

Third Year Student at Cal State University - Long Beach

| Time | Monday | Tuesday | Wednesday | Thursday | Friday |
|---|---|---|---|---|---|
| 8:00 AM | COMM 307 8:00AM - 9:15AM Hall of Science 103 | | COMM 307 8:00AM - 9:15AM Hall of Science 103 | | |
| 9:00 AM | | | | | |
| 10:00 AM | | | | | |
| 11:00 AM | COMM 421 11:00AM - 12:15PM Kinesiology 059 | | COMM 421 11:00AM - 12:15PM Kinesiology 059 | | |
| 12:00 PM | | | | | |
| 1:00 PM | | | | | |
| 2:00 PM | COMM 412 2:00PM - 3:15 PM Peterson Hall 1 140 | | COMM 412 2:00PM - 3:15 PM Peterson Hall 1 140 | | |
| 3:00 PM | | | | | |
| 4:00 PM | COMM 300 3:30PM - 4:45 PM Peterson Hall 1 140 | | COMM 300 3:30PM - 4:45 PM Peterson Hall 1 140 | | |
| 5:00 PM | | KIN 183A 5:00PM - 6:50PM Kinesiology 107 | | | |
| 6:00 PM | | | | | |
| 7:00 PM | | | | | |

Thought Box:

OK, so you can decide on your schedule. What else?

- **You can choose your classes**, many of which might truly interest you! For example, Sac State offers everything from "Intro to Hip Hop Beat-Making" and "Human Development" to "Criminology" and "Entrepreneurship." **Learning is much easier if you're actually interested in the content!**

- **You can eat happily.** Say goodbye to your crusty old cafeteria and hello to better options like Chipotle and Chick-fil-A.

- **Less quantity, more quality.** Many college courses replace nightly busy work with a few significant tests or essays due at specific points throughout the semester.

- **College can be FUN.** Making new friends, living and learning in a diverse community, watching or playing sports, participating in clubs or Greek life (fraternities/sororities), free movie screenings and concerts, road trips, and more.

- **You'll have the freedom** and responsibility of an adult in college. Teachers aren't likely to nag you about being absent or missing work. You can go out all night on a Monday if you want, eventually learning the consequences of doing so. It's all up to you.

Whatever you decide to do after high school, consider each option's pros and cons, and then take responsibility for your commitment.

**Don't go** to college just because your friends will be there or because someone else filled out an application for you.

**Go because** the benefits will outweigh the costs. **Go because** you're willing to put in the effort.

You can earn a college degree if you want it. For help getting started, type "Steps to enroll in (name of college)" into Google, meet with a counselor at your high school or college, finish this book, and make a specific plan.

# CHAPTER RECAP

1. Compared to high school, college typically offers more interesting classes, greater freedom, flexibility in your daily schedule, and more job opportunities after graduation.

2. Statistics show that college graduates are more likely to receive job offers and make more money.

3. If you're accepted, your college believes you can succeed there. Others believe in you, so believe in yourself. Don't be afraid to seek out support when you need it.

## ESSENTIAL QUESTIONS

1. What do you want from your education?

High School:

_____

_____

_____

_____

College:

_____

_____

_____

_____

2. What are you willing to sacrifice to achieve your goals?

_____

_____

_____

_____

_____

_____

3. Community College, UC, Cal State, 4-year Private University, Out-of-State Public University, Military, Trade School, Work...

What are you thinking about next? Reflect on the pros and cons of your main options in the following tables.

| Option 1: | |
|---|---|
| Pros | Cons |
| | |

| Option 2: | |
|---|---|
| Pros | Cons |
| | |

4. Before building a college plan, decide where your help and advice will come from. Is there a family member who's always been there to guide you? Can you think of any teachers, school counselors, coaches, or mentors who want to see you succeed? Do you have other friends with similar goals?

Try to find people from different areas of your life who know you well and have your best interests at heart. When you're ready, write down three names and talk to them about this book and your thoughts about college and financial aid!

| | My Team | How I Contact Them |
|---|---|---|
| #1 | | |
| #2 | | |
| #3 | | |

Blank Space Just for You

Blank Space Just for You

Blank Space Just for You... Chapter 2 Coming Up Next!

# 2

# A Good Fit

Pre-Chapter Thoughts:

1. If money had nothing to do with it, what colleges would be most attractive to you?

_____

_____

_____

_____

2. What attracts you to those colleges? Prestige? Location? Reputation? Athletics? Something else?

_____

_____

_____

_____

*(Reading this book) I have learned many things that I had no clue about...
I don't think I would be able to learn this anywhere else, so I'm really glad I
got to learn it here. - Alex S.*

If you go out to a fancy restaurant, you may use the following thought process to pick your meal:

1. Look at the prices,

2. Look at what might taste best out of the cheaper items,

3. Order.

That process may work well for a night out – you sacrificed what may have been the more enjoyable meal to save some cash.

But should you choose a college using the same thought process?

For those who say "yes," beware: many students (and adults) don't actually get #1 (looking at prices) right. Everyone at the table will pay different prices, but few do the research necessary to figure out the price they'll pay.

For those who want a more thorough thought process, going honestly and intentionally through this book will help. But reading this book is not enough. You'll also need to do some things outside of school – like use a Net Price Calculator with a parent/guardian at home, fill out the FAFSA, and apply to colleges. Only then will you clearly understand what each college will cost you.

Paying for college can take years, not minutes, and the benefits can last a *lifetime*, not a few hours like your dinner. College-related decisions should **not** be made in the same way as food- or entertainment-related decisions; college comes with *long-term* benefits and costs that require more scrutiny.

This chapter investigates the characteristics of college that are most important to you, outside of cost. These may include **academics**, **school culture**, **location**, and **class sizes**. Once we narrow down the environment you prefer to learn in, we'll walk you through college data – graduation rates, loan default rates, average net cost, and financial aid – some of which are often overlooked despite their importance. This is a journey to determine which college provides you with the greatest overall value.

## SELAH'S STORY

Selah is a 12th-grader who is excited but also nervous about college. Going from high school to college will be the most significant change in her life, so she wants to think through all her options.

Instead of only applying to schools her friends are talking about, Selah creates an outline to find the best schools for her. As she wonders, "What do I want in a school?" Here is what she comes up with:

| Important | Not as Important |
|---|---|
| Strong Academics | School Size |
| Intramural Sports | |
| In Northern or Southern California | |

As you can see, Selah's *initial* outline doesn't include how easy it may be to apply or gain admission, costs, or majors offered. Let's explore why this is a wise strategy for her...

### Why not go for the easiest application and admission?

Just because it's "easy" to apply (or get admitted) to a certain college, it may not be the right place for you. At the least selective schools (those with open admissions), only 28% of students graduated with a bachelor's degree within six years! For comparison, the 6-year graduation rate was 90% at the universities considered most selective (with an acceptance rate of less than

21

25%).[3]

Not looking at the most selective universities? Recent data show a graduation rate of over 60% for the universities that admitted 50% to 74.9%. What does all this mean to you?

---

Thought Box:

 

 

 

 

 

 

 

---

### Why not limit your college applications based on cost?

The cost of attendance on a college's website can be *dramatically different* than the price you will actually pay to attend. <u>Wait until AFTER you receive your award letter to decide if it's affordable.</u> The reason:

# FINANCIAL AID

 Have you ever seen something on sale for 50 – 100% off?! Many students with financial need receive these kinds of massive discounts for college.

---

[3] https://nces.ed.gov/programs/coe/pdf/2022/ctr_508.pdf

## Why not limit your college options based on major?

Some advisors tell students to find a major first and focus on colleges that offer (or are known for) that major. If you want to limit your college options because you have a defined career goal that you're sure about, then that's good advice.

For example, if you *know* you want to become a doctor, you need to take pre-med courses, and if you want a job as an engineer, you should probably study engineering.

Otherwise, there are three things about college majors that you should understand:

1. Most large universities offer a similar and large variety of majors.

2. Nearly one out of every three students change majors in their first three years of college.[4]

3. Many careers require a bachelor's degree but not a specific major. One of my good friends studied communications and chose a career in finance. I studied finance and switched careers to work in education. As of 2014, **only 27%** of college students ended up working in a job that was directly related to their college major.[5]

---

### YOUR TURN

Start narrowing down colleges by looking for those that will provide you with what you need most: the right *learning and social environment*. We're going to focus on academics, culture, and location. Feel free to add any others that are important to you.

---

[4] https://nces.ed.gov/pubs2018/2018434/index.asp
[5] https://www.newyorkfed.org/medialibrary/media/research/staff_reports/sr587.pdf

## ACADEMICS

What kind of academic degree do you want? Bachelors? Associates? Eventually, a J.D., M.B.A., M.A., Ph.D., M.D.? Do you want to go to a school that is well known for its academics? Do you want it to be ranked in the top 50 nationally? The top 25?

Do you want to attend a college that doesn't give letter grades? Is it more important to be somewhere that offers a curriculum completely online so you can spend more time with work, family, and friends? Do you want to go to a school that specializes in a particular career or vocation?

Academics Thought Box:

# CULTURE

Does the school host job fairs and provide enough advisors? What do potential employers think of your school? Do you enjoy spending one-on-one time with your teachers? Could you succeed in a class with 350 other people? (Check out the student-to-faculty ratio.[6])

Do you want a school that interacts with its community by planning events off-campus and inviting community leaders to speak on campus? Do you like intramural sports? Student government? Looking forward to cheering on your team as they compete for a national championship? Eager to run the campus radio station or join the marching band? Want to keep it real with other students in a religious or social activist group? Curious about joining a fraternity or sorority?

Some schools offer opportunities to explore these experiences, but many do not. Think about your ideal college experience outside the classroom, see what's available, and narrow down your college list accordingly.

Culture Thought Box:

---

[6] To do this on the College Navigator, use the search bar, and choose a college. Near the top, you will see the student to faculty ratio. https://nces.ed.gov/collegenavigator/

## LOCATION

Do you want to live in a "college town," a big city, or at home with your parents? Do you want to be able to drive home on a weekend if needed? Or would you prefer to move to that state you visited once on vacation, and it felt like home? Do you prefer the city or the countryside? As you begin this new phase in life, what's the best geographical location for you?

Location Thought Box:

## CHAPTER RECAP

1. Before looking at costs, narrow down your college choices based on who you are and what you want.

2. If you're not sure what you want to do, don't worry too much about your major. Choose to study something that you're curious about. Also, remember it's fairly common for college students to change majors.

# ESSENTIAL QUESTIONS

1. What three things do you value most in a potential school?

| #1. | |
|-----|---|
| #2. | |
| #3. | |

2. Next, let's build a list of schools that match your preferences.[7]

| Colleges | |
|-----|---|
| #1. | |
| #2. | |
| #3. | |
| #4. | |
| #5. | |
| #6. | |
| #7. | |
| #8. | |
| #9 | |
| #10 | |

---

[7] **For help:** If you've already got a few schools in mind, use this (https://www.cappex.com/colleges/) but if you still need to narrow down your search, use the filter in this link (https://bigfuture.col legeboard.org/find-colleges/how-to-find-your-college-fit/college search-step-by-step).

**3.** Label your colleges according to your likelihood of being admitted.

| | Colleges | Label (Safety/Match/Reach) |
|---|---|---|
| #1. | | |
| #2. | | |
| #3. | | |
| #4. | | |
| #5. | | |
| #6. | | |
| #7. | | |
| #8. | | |
| #9 | | |
| #10 | | |

**For help:** Log in to bigfuture.collegeboard.org and type each college listed above into the search bar. Once you're on the main page for a given college, select "Go to Academic Tracker" in the right-hand column. Once there, you can select the "How Do I Stack Up?" tab to see where you are within their GPA and SAT/ACT ranges.

Based on where you find yourself, label schools as:

- "Safety" (your GPA and test scores are well above the range),

- "Match" (your GPA and test scores are within the range), and

- "Reach" (your GPA and test scores are at the lower end or below the range) schools.

(Remember that these are only ranges—people can be above or below the range and still be accepted.)

**4.** Now rank schools according to your preferences for academics, culture, location, and school size. You don't need to use all the schools you listed previously, and you can rank the same college in more than one category.

For example, if Sac State is your best academic and cultural fit, list it in the number 1 spot for categories.

| Academics |
| --- |
| #1. |
| #2. |
| #3. |

| Culture |
| --- |
| #1. |
| #2. |
| #3. |

| Location |
| --- |
| #1. |
| #2. |
| #3. |

**5.** It's time to choose schools that will become the focus of your research throughout this book. Select your favorite Safety, Match, and Reach schools.

| Focus Schools | |
|---|---|
| **Safety:** | |
| **Match:** | |
| **Reach:** | |

Blank Space for you to think about...

What do you like and dislike about these schools?

Why would this school be lucky to have you as a student?

What can you achieve at this school that you could not achieve elsewhere?

More Blank Space for you...

# 3

# Get What You Pay For

Pre-Chapter Thoughts:

1. Earning a college degree can be a valuable experience and a lifelong asset. Describe how.

_____

_____

_____

_____

2. Have you ever paid a higher price for something because it brings greater benefits than the cheaper option?  Why did you make the purchase?

_____

_____

_____

_____

*I was afraid that the price of college would weigh me down for the rest of my life. This project showed me that this doesn't have to be the case. - Mark O.*

As we've discussed in earlier chapters, college can be one of the most valuable investments of your life. The experiences, the friends, the curriculum, the professional network, the job opportunities, etc. So, what's it worth to you? Do all colleges have the same value? How do you figure out what each college degree is worth?

Thought Box:

Hopefully, you agree that not all college experiences and degrees are worth the same. In the previous chapter, we looked at colleges that provide you with the academics, location, and culture you want. Now, we'll see if those colleges provide the student outcomes you want.

What are ideal student outcomes?

1. You graduate on time.
2. You have a job you desire after graduation.
3. You're able to afford any student loan payments after graduating.

Let's dive in.

# GRADUATION RATE

Labeling something "expensive" or "cheap" depends on what you're buying.

- $10 for one piece of lined paper? Super expensive.

- $10,000 for a Ferrari? Super cheap.

But is $10,000 cheap for college? What about $40,000? What should college cost? The answer is: **it depends**. Grouping all colleges together and saying one price is right is like saying that all basketball games should cost the same – whether the ticket is courtside at the NBA finals or in the bleachers at a regular-season high school game. Should tickets to Taylor Swift cost the same as your middle school's talent show?

With a little more in-depth research, you'll uncover more about the value each college provides its students. One of those measures of value is whether students graduate.

Graduation rates can vary from the low single digits (2% means that only 2 out of every 100 students graduate!)[8] to nearly 100%. On average, graduation rates (within eight years of entering the school) at community colleges are 32%, while graduation rates within eight years at 4-year colleges are 58%.[9]

This should be obvious: when you pay for college, you want a good chance of graduating. Are you surprised that colleges with 2% graduation rates exist?

Thought Box:

---

[8] Who has a 2% graduation rate? University of Phoenix - Arizona students (within 4 years of starting).
https://nces.ed.gov/collegenavigator/?q=phoenix&s=all&pg=2&id=484613#retgrad

[9] https://collegescorecard.ed.gov/

The **length of time** it takes to graduate is also something you want to consider when thinking about graduation. If a cheaper college "only" costs you $5,000 per year but takes *eight years* to graduate, your final college costs $40,000. That's a much higher cost than what you first estimated.

On the other hand, let's say you went to another college that cost $9,000 per year. If you graduate within four years, you will pay $4,000 less overall, and you can start a full-time job three years sooner! Graduating sooner means tuition payments stop and earning full-time money begins. 22 to 27-year-old workers with bachelor's degrees make **66% more per year** (about $24,000 more) compared to those who are the same age with high school diplomas.[10]

Let me be clear: I'm not saying that more expensive colleges *always* offer better opportunities to graduate. Students at the University of Phoenix (a private, for-profit school) pay high prices (often close to $15,000 per year without housing and food) but have one of the lowest graduation rates – 2% at one of its campuses within four years!![11] No matter how cheap a college seems, it's unlikely to be worth it if you don't graduate!

**Your Turn:** Click the "Graduation & Retention" drop-down menu on the College Scorecard. Keep in mind, the graduation rate listed here is within eight years. That's 200% of "normal time" at a four-year university and 400% of normal time at a community college. To find graduation rates within normal time or separated by gender or race/ethnicity, use the College Navigator.

| My Focus Colleges | Graduation Rates |
|---|---|
|  |  |
|  |  |
|  |  |

---

[10] "The Labor Market for Recent College Graduates," The Federal Reserve Bank of New York," 2022.
[11] https://nces.ed.gov/collegenavigator/?q=phoenix&s=all&pg=2&id=484613#retgrad

How do you feel about the graduation rates you found?

Thought Box:

If you're wondering, the reasons for low graduation rates vary widely.[12] Can students easily register for classes they need? Does it have a learning environment that feels supportive? Do students have access to free or affordable tutoring? Do academic advisors have enough time to spend helping each student understand what they need to stay on track? Remember that **you won't receive a refund if you don't graduate.**

No matter where you go, you should create a timeline and a plan for how you'll reach your goals in school. Remind yourself of the reasons you're there and that it's okay to make mistakes. Make changes to your plan as you go, and hold yourself accountable. Find a family member, friend, mentor, professor, or anyone who's been there before and can support you along the way.

## TRANSFERRING

Many community college students expect to transfer to a 4-year college for their last two years of schooling. Yes, you'll likely save some money taking your general education classes at a community college, but don't assume it's easy to transfer when/how you want. According to a report from the Public Policy Institute of California, just 10% of transfer-intending students actually transfer in two years or less, and 19% transfer within four years.[13]

---

[12] https://files.eric.ed.gov/fulltext/ED507432.pdf
[13] https://www.ppic.org/publication/strengthening-californias-transfer-pathway/

Transfer plans are not carried out as often as you might expect. Time to do some research. Use the College Navigator (google "College Navigator" to find the site) and select the "Retention and Graduation Rate" drop-down to find your local community college's transfer rate within two years. Then, go to the College Scorecard (different site) to find the published transfer rate (within eight years).

| Local Community College | Transfer Rate (2 year) | Transfer Rate (8 year) |
|---|---|---|
|  |  |  |

Thought Box:

What can you do to successfully transfer? To transfer to a UC, look into the Transfer Admission Guarantee "TAG" program.[14] To transfer to a Cal

---

14
https://admission.universityofcalifornia.edu/admission-requirements/transfer-requirements/uc-transfer-programs/transfer-admission-guarantee-tag.html

State, create a specific, achievable plan using their online Transfer Planner.[15] If you're planning to transfer from a 2-year to a 4-year university, see the Deeper Dive section toward the end of this book to create a plan.

## LOAN DEFAULT RATE

As I've already suggested, going to college should result in earning a degree, which should then result in a job that provides an income. Yes, it's true Bill Gates and Mark Zuckerberg didn't *need* their Harvard degrees. If you have the ideas, skills, and grit to create the next Microsoft or Facebook, then sure, go the same route.

But for every billionaire tech visionary drop-out, there are millions who drop out and get jobs they could've taken right out of high school.

If you borrow money for college, you *should* be able to use some of your future income to repay what you borrowed.

**Q:** When will I need to repay my student loans?

**A:** You don't need to pay your loans while you're still in school! Your repayment period begins soon after students graduate or drop below half-time enrollment. Unfortunately, some students don't repay the money they borrowed, meaning they **default** on their loans.[16]

Defaulting is **not good**. It crushes the borrower's credit score. The lender can also garnish wages (take money out of the borrower's paycheck) and take any tax refunds owed to the borrower.[17]

When researching universities, you want them to have low (ideally zero) default rates, meaning their graduates have successfully managed their student loan payments. Check out the following table which shows loan default rates at various private and public colleges.

---

[15] https://www.calstate.edu/apply/transfer
[16] More on student loans in Chapter 6.
[17] Read more about the consequences of default here: https://studentaid.gov/manage-loans/default

| College | Loan Default Rates |
|---|---|
| Pomona College | 0% |
| UC Davis | 2% |
| Sac State | 4% |
| University of Phoenix - Arizona | 11% |

**Your Turn:** Look under the Financial Aid & Debt tab at your focus schools' College Scorecard Profile and complete the table below.

| My Focus Colleges | Loan Default Rates |
|---|---|
|  |  |
|  |  |
|  |  |

Why do people default on their student loans?

_____

_____

_____

What do you think of the default rates at your focus schools?

_____

_____

_____

If you borrow for college, how can you avoid default?

More on loans, interest rates, and credit in Chapter 6.

## CHAPTER RECAP

1. Don't limit your options to colleges you "think" are affordable until after you've received college acceptances with financial aid award letters.

2. Some students will still pay the full price (sometimes $60,000), while others will pay significantly less (maybe $0) for the same university. It all depends on the grants and scholarships offered.

3. Be sure to look up graduation rates and loan default rates before choosing a college. It may make sense to pay a higher price for college if it provides greater benefits and/or a better experience!

4. As you plan for college, it's essential you have a realistic expectation of how many years it will take you to graduate. Use the **College Navigator** (online) to find "normal time" graduation rates (two or four years) and the **College Scorecard** to find the percentage of students graduating within eight years.

## ESSENTIAL QUESTIONS

1. How important (scale of 1-10) will graduation rates, transfer rates, and loan default rates be as you look into applying to college?

Grad Rates:

Transfer Rates:

Loan Default Rates:

2. Why did you rank each at the importance level above?

Blank Space Just for You

Blank Space Just for You

# 4

# Free Money Part 1

Pre-Chapter Thoughts:

1. What do you think students pay on average for in-state tuition and fees at a 4-year Public University?

2. What do you think students pay on average for tuition and fees at a 4-year Private University?

3. Who (people, governments, companies, institutions?) will help you pay for college?

_____

_____

_____

_____

_____

*Through research for this project, I saw that there are many different scholarships from around the U.S. that I can apply for, which may award anything from $100 to a full ride to the college I go to. - Joel L.*

No matter who you are, it's possible to afford 4-year and 2-year colleges. To make it happen, you need money. If you (or your family) cannot pay for college, you can receive financial aid to help. In the world of financial aid, these are the main options:

1. **Student Loans:** Money you borrow and pay back later. Student loans can be good or bad, depending on the costs and benefits involved. We'll discuss loans in more detail in Chapter 6.

2. **Grants and Scholarships:** Money you don't have to pay back. This "free money" is the best type of aid, and it's our focus for this chapter. You can get this type of financial aid because of who you are, what you've done, and where you come from.

To receive financial aid, you'll need to complete some of the applications we cover in Chapters 7 and 8. For now, let's get a better understanding of the two major aid categories: need-based aid and merit-based aid.

## NEED-BASED AID

Need-based aid includes *grants*, *work-study*, and *loans*. You apply by submitting the FAFSA and possibly the CSS Profile.[18] These applications inform colleges and the state and federal governments how much your family can afford to pay for college. If you're undocumented, you can still qualify for need-based aid from the state of CA and your university by filling out the CA Dream Act Application.[19]

Shortly after you get accepted to each college, you'll receive a financial aid "award letter" that lists all offers of need-based aid.[20] After receiving your award letter, you can accept the aid you want and decline the aid you don't want.

---

[18] Chapter 7 covers the FAFSA and CSS Profile in depth.
[19] Chapter 8 covers the Dream Act in depth.
[20] Check out some example award letters here: https://ncs.uchicago.edu/tool/example-financial-aid-award-letters

45

Obviously, you should always accept the grants offered – they are free money!

Here are some details about the most popular need-based forms of aid (not including loans) available .

**1.**

**Federal Grants:** The most popular grant from the U.S. government is called the *Pell Grant*.

The maximum Pell Grant amount each student can get for the 2017-2018 school year is $7,395.[21] Other federal grants include the FESOG, TEACH, and Service Grants.[22]

**Federal Work-Study:** Many colleges also offer a type of federal need-based aid called work-study. Work-study provides students with advantages in landing part-time jobs on or near campus. If you qualify for work-study, you can search for jobs once you arrive on campus. These jobs are usually easy to apply for and have flexible hours based on your class schedule.

Quick story: I was offered work-study at USC and found a job in our school newspaper, the Daily Trojan. I didn't need any prior work experience to apply, and the job was located on campus, a few buildings away from most of my classes. It was a great way to work while going to school. And unlike other types of financial aid, this money was given to me in the form of a paycheck. I could spend it on books, tuition, gas for my car, or a milkshake for my friend. The decision was mine.

Would you take work-study if it was offered? Explain.

Thought Box:

---

[21] https://studentaid.gov/understand-aid/types/grants/pell
[22] https://studentaid.gov/understand-aid/types/grants

**State Grants:** Another source of free money: state governments! Cal Grants can total up to:

- $7,390 at CSUs,
- $15,400 at UCs, and
- $11,006 at Private Non-Profit Schools.[23]

One great thing about the Cal Grant is that the application is easy! No essays or tests are involved.

Here is what you need to do:[24]

1. File the FAFSA or CA Dream Act Application. (You should already be doing this anyway...) These forms prove that you need the money.

2. Next, submit a GPA Verification Form with the help of your high school. Check in with your high school counselor to make sure you get this done on time. (Public high schools and public charter schools must submit this information during your senior year, but double-check with your counselor to make sure yours is sent.)

3. Create a "WEBGRANTS 4 STUDENTS" Account online. See the Cal Grant Website for more information.

Here's a quote from Diana Fuentes-Michel, retired Executive Director of the California Student Aid Commission.

"As the oldest sibling in a Latino family, a Cal Grant made it easier for me to talk with my family about the possibility of going to college. The Cal Grant Program made college a reality for me and my siblings... For myself, I really attribute my ability to go to graduate school and become a leader in higher education policy to the Cal Grant Program. There is no way I'd be here without it."

---

[23] https://www.csac.ca.gov/post/what-are-cal-grant-award-amounts
[24] https://www.csac.ca.gov/how-apply

## 3

**University Grants:** Out of the $145 billion in grant aid given to students in 2022-23, 53% of it came from universities – that's the largest source of financial aid that doesn't need to be repaid![25]

Some universities even have financial aid programs known as *no-loan aid*. No loan aid means students get a financial aid package that will cover all college costs if their family falls into a specific income range.

Yes, this means **FREE COLLEGE!**

Some hecklers complain that students still have to take out loans even though they qualify for a no-loan aid program. But this is like getting a free ticket, drink, and pretzel for a basketball game and then complaining that you have to buy your own dessert. After all, the total amount of money needed for college depends not just on tuition, room, and board but also on your lifestyle and willingness to hold a part-time job.

Haters aside, no-loan aid programs offer incredibly generous discounts. They provide access to college for students who otherwise wouldn't be able to afford it. If you get accepted to a school with a no-loan policy and your family makes less than a certain amount — usually somewhere between $40,000 and $150,000 annually — some good aid awaits. Your final cost of college will be much more affordable than you think.

You might ask yourself, "How can all these universities afford to give away so much money?" They have $$$. Every year, many of these universities receive massive donations from community leaders who want to support education. Not all donations help pay for undergraduate education, but they do allow universities more room in their budgets to give students huge amounts of financial aid.

---

[25] The College Board, Trends in College Pricing and Financial Aid.
https://research.collegeboard.org/trends/student-aid

**Recently:**

- John Paulson, a hedge fund manager, donated $400 million to Harvard.

- Nike founder Phil Knight gave $500 million to Oregon Health and Science University.

- Music moguls Dr. Dre and Jimmy Iovine (who sold Beats headphones to Apple) donated $70 million for a new major at USC.

Universities with no-loan aid policies include very competitive private schools like Harvard, Princeton, Brown, Caltech, Columbia, Dartmouth, Duke, and Stanford. Other excellent schools that offer similar programs include the UCs, the University of Florida, the University of Arizona, Boston University, Texas A&M, and the University of Michigan, to name a few. Just a heads up, though, some schools restrict no-loan aid to in-state students. Be sure to check their policies before applying.

Learn more about no-loan aid and the universities that offer them.[26] List any no-loan universities that you might consider.

| No-loan Universities I Might Consider |
| --- |
|  |
|  |
|  |

---

[26] https://blog.collegevine.com/no-loan-colleges-what-they-are-and-a-complete-list

# Free Money Part 2

1. What makes you unique? Do you (or your family) belong to a group that may provide scholarships? Have you done anything unique in your school or local community?

_____

_____

_____

_____

2. How much work are you willing to do when applying for scholarships? (e.g., write a 2000-word essay? Make a prom dress out of duct tape?)

_____

_____

_____

_____

# MERIT-BASED AID

In addition to the billions of dollars in need-based aid given to students each year, billions more are given away in the form of merit-based aid, usually known as scholarships. Scholarships are just as excellent as grants because the money never needs to be repaid.

Here's the catch: you don't typically receive scholarships without some work on your part. Be prepared to write an essay and get letters of recommendation from teachers, counselors, and mentors in your life. Don't give up too quickly – you probably have a better chance of getting the scholarship if there *is* a lot of work to do. More work (such as writing a 2,000-word essay and getting three letters of recommendation) will filter out thousands of people who don't want to do the work.

Essays and letters of recommendation also allow you to fully explain your story and show why you are an excellent candidate for the scholarship money. There are scholarships with a career focus, like the NURSE Corps Scholarship Program, which pays for all of your education.[27] Some scholarships provide students with academic, personal, and financial support throughout college, like The Posse Foundation[28] and The Jackie Robinson Foundation.[29]

Of course, these scholarships aren't the only ones in town. There are thousands of scholarships out there. Think of it this way: there's probably a scholarship for every interest you have. Do you play sports? Scholarship. Are you involved in the arts? Scholarship. Did you make your Prom outfit out of Duck Tape®? Scholarship. (Seriously, visit stuckatprom.com). You get the idea.

Anything, from your extracurricular activities to your religion and your ethnicity, can be potential scholarship opportunities. It's time to find the money available to you because of the awesome person you are!

List 3 – 5 scholarships you may qualify for, and describe why you would be a good candidate. **For help** – Check out what scholarships are available to

---

[27] http://www.hrsa.gov/loanscholarships/scholarships/Nursing/
[28] https://www.possefoundation.org/
[29] https://www.jackierobinson.org/

you using any of these links: Going Merry (goingmerry.com), College Board (https://bigfuture.collegeboard.org/scholarship-search), Fastweb (fastweb.com).

It's often wise to start local (within your school), then look within your school district, then your city, county, state, and national. Be sure to ask your high school counselor for the names of local scholarships that students from your high school have received in past years.

| Scholarship Name | Description and $ Amount | Application Deadline |
| --- | --- | --- |
| | | |
| | | |
| | | |
| | | |
| | | |

## BEWARE SCAMS!!

You should NEVER have to pay money (even as low as $1.00) to access or apply for a scholarship. <u>Never</u> put credit card information down, provide your FAFSA info (anywhere other than the studentaid.gov website), or commit to anything that claims it will "do all the work for you."

## ON AVERAGE, DO STUDENTS REALLY GET FINANCIAL AID?

You've probably heard that the total costs of college (tuition, fees, room, and board) have grown sharply over the past decade. But most people don't know that the average net tuition and fees actually paid by in-state students in public four-year universities **DECLINED** (from a peak of $4,230 in 2012-13) to an estimated $2,730 in 2023-24. Students enrolled in private nonprofit four-year universities **ALSO DECLINED** from $18,820 (in 2023 dollars) in 2006-07 to an estimated $15,910 in 2023-24.[30]

# There's more financial aid available today compared to the past.

Time to look at the prices students actually pay (for tuition, fees, housing, food, books, supplies, etc.) for college after taking into account the billions of dollars of grants and scholarships they receive – a number better known as the **net price.**

To show the math, the image on the right shows what a student in a family of five with parents earning $100,000 per year might pay for a private 4-year university in Southern California (Claremont McKenna).

| Estimated Cost of Attendance | |
|---|---|
| Tuition & Fees | $65,714 |
| Food & Housing | $20,240 |
| Books, Course Materials, Supplies, and Equipment | $1,200 |
| Transportation | $150 |
| Miscellaneous Personal Expenses | $1,500 |
| Total | $88,804 |
| | |
| Estimated Grant/Gift Aid | |
| Claremont McKenna College Grant | $74,600 |
| | |
| **Estimated NET PRICE** | **$14,204** |

---

[30] Adjusted for inflation. https://research.collegeboard.org/trends/college-pricing/highlights

What does this show? The gross price ("Total") is $88,804 per year, and this student will receive a grant (money they never need to repay) of $74,600 per year. This means the student has a net price of $14,204 per year.

They can still reduce this by buying used books and being frugal with their "personal expenses." (To put this in perspective, I typed the same student details in for Sac State and got a net price of over $20,000 per year...)

Thought Box:

How can the student pay the remaining $14,000 if they don't get financial help from their parents? They can work about 15 hours per week.

Now it's time to research the universities you're considering by looking at the *average* net prices students pay. In the next chapter, you'll get an even more accurate estimate of your **personal net price** by finding a college's net price calculator and filling out a few financial details.

For now, go to the College Scorecard[31] (online) to find the **average annual cost (i.e., net price)**. Remember these are the averages; some students will still pay the full (gross) price, while others will pay less (maybe $0) *for the same education at the same university*. It all depends on the financial aid a student receives.

---

[31] The College Scorecard displays college-related data collected by The U.S. Department of Education

Use the Focus Schools you found in Chapter 2 to complete the following table.

| My Focus Schools | Average Annual Cost |
|---|---|
|  |  |
|  |  |
|  |  |

Thought Box:

With more financial aid, we've seen an increase in students from low-income backgrounds attending colleges once considered much too expensive. But, *many* students still don't know about all the financial aid opportunities available to them.[32] Here's some important college application advice I mentioned earlier:

---

[32] Long, B. "The New Financial Aid Policies: Their Impact on Access and Equity For Low-Income Students?" Harvard Graduate School of Education (2010). 15-16.

**Wait until *after* you've received financial aid award letters to decide if a college is too expensive.**

Highlight that. Share it with your neighbor. If you really want to attend a particular college, apply! Go for it. And if someone tells you that you won't be able to afford it, ask yourself:

Is the person telling you that a financial aid officer at the university you're applying to?

- If so, do they have your financial aid application in hand?
- If not, **they don't have all the information necessary to tell you what you can and cannot afford.**

You are unique, and financial aid is different from student to student. It's very common for students to pay different prices for the same college. If your financial aid award letter still isn't enough, see the additional steps you can take in the "Extras" portion of the back of this book.

---

### The Story of the Expensive Private School

Stanford is one of those "exclusive private universities" with a gross price of over $90,000 annually. That might seem extremely expensive, but this is what actually happens on campus:

- The **average scholarship** for the current (class of 2027) Stanford freshmen class **is over $70,000**.

- If a student's family earns between $100,000 - $125,000 per year, Stanford (including tuition, food, housing, and other costs) will cost $13,201 on average!

  You will spend more on housing and food if you're living on your own and *not* going to college.[33]

---

[33] https://financialaid.stanford.edu/undergrad/how/index.html

Stanford has extremely selective admissions, making it a challenge to get in. However, its financial aid policy shows how some "expensive" private schools become cheaper than state schools when financial aid is considered.

## OTHER WAYS TO MAKE COLLEGE AFFORDABLE

### Sam and West Coast Reduced Tuition

 Sam is a student from San Diego who dreams of attending the University of Arizona. Tuition for Arizona residents is $13,900. Unfortunately, Sam is not from Arizona. He assumes he'll need to pay non-resident tuition, around $42,300.

Instead of giving up on his dream, Sam is determined to get his price reduced. Using the world's best library (Google), Sam soon finds a program called the Western Undergraduate Exchange (WUE).[34] Since Sam lives in the Western U.S. and U of A participates in WUE, he can get the massive discount that comes with WUE: 150% of the *resident* tuition rate.

Sam did the math and found that his tuition at U of A would decrease to $20,850 with WUE![35] His new cost is less than half of what he originally thought he would have to pay. Sam is fired up!

Knowing about this program is not enough to get Sam the reduced tuition. He still needs to check the 'WUE' box on U of A's online application. If there isn't one, he'll need to reach out to the Admissions Office and ask them how he can apply for it. Some colleges give WUE reduced tuition on a first-come, first-served basis, so Sam better get his application in early!

---

[34] https://www.wiche.edu/tuition-savings/wue/
[35] $13,900*1.5 = $20,850

# QuestBridge

An organization that connects low-income students with 37 of the nation's best universities, QuestBridge[36] allows students to match college admission with significant scholarships that cover 100% of their financial need. Here is a quote from QuestBridge's mission statement:

*"QuestBridge connects high-achieving students from low-income backgrounds with a thriving community and transformative educational, career, and life opportunities that help propel them to lives of fulfillment, meaning, and purpose."*

## Starbucks: A Job that Pays!

Here's one more awesome way to get free tuition: In 2015, Starbucks introduced the Starbucks College Achievement Plan.[37] If Starbucks hires you and you work an average of 20 hours a week, you become immediately eligible to receive <u>free tuition </u>at Arizona State University. BOOOOM!

The degree you'll earn is the real deal: it's the same diploma as those who attend courses in person, and you can attend the graduation ceremony with all the other ASU seniors when you finish.

Didn't get hired at the Starbucks down the street? Just go another few miles down the road and apply again!!

## The Military

Over 1000 colleges have Reserve Officer Training Corps (ROTC) programs offered by the U.S. Army, Navy, and Air Force. ROTC is an excellent option for students to get some (or all) of college paid for while committing to military service after graduating. If this is an opportunity that interests you, visit: http://todaysmilitary.com/training/rotc.

## Live On The Cheap

Room, board, and other living expenses could quickly add up to over $10,000 annually. If you'd like to lower these costs, the first option is to eat

---

[36] https://www.questbridge.org/
[37] https://starbucks.asu.edu/

cheap (think mac and cheese) and choose the lowest-cost dorm, or maybe consider living at home. During my sophomore year at USC, my roommate and I shared a room the size of a utility closet, and it worked out just fine. You can also buy used books and choose cheap transportation options to help lower your living expenses.

If you're looking to save even more, see if your college has a co-op program where you can work to pay off your tuition. Co-ops typically look different than work-study because you might alternate between school and work for 6-month cycles. Your college might also have a nearby co-op housing program. This is where affordable housing is offered to co-op members, who share resources and responsibilities associated with the housing complex.

Or, if you want to stay on campus, you can also apply to become a Resident Advisor. As an "RA," you get free or reduced housing based on your work, maintenance, and supervision of students in a residence hall.

### The American Opportunity Tax Credit

You can get a tax credit (tax money put back in your pocket) of up to $2,500 based on college expenses. As a college student, you'll typically receive a tax form (1098-T) by mail from your school each January. This form will help you figure out your tax credit.

When filing your taxes for the previous year, you'll need to complete Form 8863 and attach it to your Form 1040 or Form 1040A. Sound complicated? Is the work worth a few thousand dollars in your pocket? When it comes time to file taxes, follow the instructions and links included here:

https://www.irs.gov/credits-deductions/individuals/aotc

### CHAPTER RECAP

1. While every student might not be able to afford every college, every student can find one they can afford.

2. By filling out the FAFSA, you may get all or some of the following:

a. federal, state, and university grants (money you don't have to repay)

b. work-study (a flexible job on or near campus)

c. student loans from the federal government (see Chapter 6 for more on loans)

3. More than 100 universities around the country have no-loan aid programs, which cover college costs for students who demonstrate a need for such financial support.

4. Ideally, you want to apply for financial aid from all directions — the federal government, state government, your university, and any other private foundation.

5. NEVER pay for a scholarship. Don't put credit card information down, provide your FAFSA info, or commit to anything that claims it will "do all the work for you."

6. The military and corporations like Starbucks also offer significant financial support for college in exchange for your work.

Blank Space Just For You...

Blank Space Just For You...

# 5

# Your Cost to Attend College

Pre-Chapter Thoughts:

1. Would you prefer to attend a two-year or four-year college if cost wasn't an issue? Why?

_____

_____

_____

_____

_____

_____

_____

_____

*Now, I am striving harder to get in, knowing that the only thing holding me back is my performance. I can no longer have the excuse of lacking funds because this project showed me that it is not usually the case. - Mark Z.*

So far, we've seen the lifetime benefits of a college degree and looked into the key elements to consider when choosing a college. We know the massive amounts of life-changing financial aid available, and we know what other students pay, on average, to attend different colleges. And now it's your turn. **It's time you get the most realistic estimate of *your* net price to attend college.**

How can you do this? By answering a few questions online on a **net price calculator**. Nearly every college has one. Depending on your family's financial situation, you may be surprised to see you will likely get a BIG financial aid award. For example, the UC System's "Blue and Gold Opportunity Plan" covers *all tuition and fees* if your family makes less than $80,000 per year.[38]

Net price calculators are free, and you can calculate as many different financial scenarios as you want, though you should be as accurate as possible. Keep in mind: these calculators don't account for other scholarships you may receive, so lace up and find more ways to lower your final cost even further.

## JORDAN AND THE UC NPC

Jordan was thinking about attending UC Irvine and decided to check out their net price calculator to figure out what it might cost him to attend. Here are the details he entered into the calculator:

- Jordan entered his parents' income – about $90,000 per year, paid $15,000 in taxes
- His parents have assets (cash and investments) worth about $75,000.
- Last year, Jordan made about $5,700 working at a movie theater. He

has $1000 in assets (cash).

- Jordan has two siblings, including one who will be in college at the same time as him.
- He also wants to live on campus since living on campus is awesome.
- Jordan is considered a dependent. Most students graduating from high school will apply for financial aid as dependents. If you are curious if you might qualify as an independent, look here:

https://studentaid.ed.gov/sa/fafsa/filling-out/dependency

Before using a net price calculator, Jordan never thought he could afford college. But now, for the first time, he realizes it is a possibility.

Check out Jordan's results:

*UCI Net Price Calculator – Dependent*[2]

| Estimated Total Cost of Attendance *without* Financial Aid | |
|---|---|
| Tuition and Fees | $15,835.93 |
| Room (housing) and Board (food) | + $16,561 |
| Books and Supplies | + $1,361 |
| Other Expenses | + $2284 |
| **Total Cost of Attendance** | **$36,041.93** |

| Estimated Financial Aid and Net Price | |
|---|---|
| Grants | $18,827 – $19,827 |
| **Estimated Net Price** | **$16,214 – $17,214** |

After accounting for financial aid provided by UCI, the University expects Jordan and his family to come up with between $16,214 - $17,214 instead of

$36,041! That's a discount of about $20,000 from the sticker price!

In the end, Jordan could cover this $16,000 cost with a combination of support from parents, additional scholarships, work-study or another part-time job, his own savings, and if necessary, loans.

Thought Box:


What Questions Do You Have?


## JESSICA AND THE HARVEY MUDD NPC

After graduating from high school, Jessica wants to continue living with her mom so that she can help out with her three younger siblings. Her single mom earns $45,000 annually, and she has no older siblings in college.

Given her situation, she got this result from the Net Price Calculator for Harvey Mudd, a private 4-year university in Southern California:

| Estimated Total Cost of Attendance *without* Financial Aid | |
| --- | --- |
| Tuition and Fees | $68,863 |
| Room (housing) and Board (food) | + $22,318 |
| Books and Supplies | + $800 |
| Other Expenses | + $1,600 |
| **Total Cost of Attendance** | **$93,581** |

| Estimated Financial Aid and Net Price | |
| --- | --- |
| Grants | $85,445 |
| **Estimated Net Price** | **$8,136** |

Based on her family income, Jessica's "Estimated net price" to attend CSULB is only $8,136. Awesome! She can cover that amount with a loan or, even better, a job or additional scholarships. This includes her housing and food for the year!

Thought Box:

You might think - "ok, but my parents make more than the Jordan and Jessica examples." If we switched Jessica's situation to where her mom earned $175,000 per year and had $100,000 in investments, this is what her net price would look like:

*Harvey Mudd Net Price Calculator* - $175,000 Income

| Estimated Financial Aid and Net Price | |
|---|---|
| Grants | $76,200 |
| **Estimated Net Price** | **$17,381** |

WOW! Not too bad, considering her family income is more than three times greater than the earlier example!

Remember, these are estimates — if you don't apply for the aid, you're not going to get it. You need to complete the applications before the deadlines and possibly do additional work on your end. You might have to write an essay, get a job on campus, or keep a minimum GPA (usually 3.0, sometimes 3.5).

Also, this financial aid is an estimate for one year in school. You have to reapply for *most* need-based aid each year. So, if your family situation changes while you're in college, your financial aid situation will also likely change, for better or worse.

I wish net price calculators had been available to me when I was applying to college in 2002. If I had known the generous amount of financial aid USC was about to offer me, I would have been way less stressed!

**Attention to Detail**

It's important to remember that net price calculators are found *directly* on each university's website. They *do not* ask for your name, social security number, FSA ID, or home address. However, they *do* ask for your family's annual income, and some will require additional information about taxes and assets.

Nobody checks this information for accuracy on the calculator (again, they don't ask for your name), so it's up to you to input the correct numbers. Obviously, the more accurate the information you provide, the more accurate the price estimate. This may be a good time to have an honest discussion with your parents regarding your family's financial situation so you can get a realistic look at your college costs.

*If your parents are divorced, separated, or remarried, please go to this link for guidance on whose information you'll use to estimate your financial aid: http://studentaid.ed.gov/fafsa/filling-out/parent info.

**If your parents are unavailable or don't want to input their information for this exercise, please use the median information for your community, which can be found at http://www.city-data.com/.

When applying for financial aid in real life (as we will cover in Chapter 7), you *will* need your parents to input their personal financial information.

### Your Turn

Using Google is the easiest way to find net price calculators, though they're also linked on the College Scorecard. Here's an example of what to type into Google: "UCLA net price calculator."

Write your net price (the amount you'll be expected to pay after financial aid is applied) for each of your focus schools in the table below. Since this information is personal, you should not be required to share it with anyone else.

| School Name | My Net Price |
|---|---|
| 1. | |
| 2. | |
| 3. | |

## CHAPTER RECAP

Net price calculators are eye-opening. USE THEM. They're free to use as many times as you want, and they provide you with a more accurate description of what it costs to attend different colleges.

Blank Space Just for You

# 6

# How to Borrow (Wisely)

Pre-Chapter Thoughts:

1. Do you think you'll likely need to borrow money for college? Explain.

_____

_____

_____

_____

2. Describe a situation after college where the monthly payment of your student loans would be affordable for you.

_____

_____

_____

_____

_____

*The most interesting thing I have learned in this financial aid project is definitely the loan forgiveness plan. I definitely think I can afford college much more now than in the past. My mind is more at ease about paying for college... - McKenna B.*

Borrowing money often comes with too much stress and too little awareness. Why don't we teach high school students how loans work?

Today, we do.

## Question 1: Why would I ever want to use a student loan?

Depending on what you're buying, debt can be a helpful tool. There are many good reasons why people (even billionaires[39]), companies, and governments borrow money.

- You might want to own a home,

- Domino's might want to open up a new store down the street,

- California's government might want to build a bridge.

In each case, the person making the final decision should thoroughly explore *all* costs and benefits involved. You should do the same when deciding how to pay for **college - one of the most significant investments in your life.**

---

Thought Box: Describe a time when you, or someone you know, benefited from borrowing money.

---

[39] http://www.npr.org/sections/thetwo-way/2012/07/16/156849011/a-perk of-being-rich-facebooks-zuckerberg-pays-1-percent-interest-on-mortgage

## Question 2: Will I have to pay for student loans while I'm still in college?

Payments on student loans from the federal government[40] don't begin until after your "grace period" expires: 6 months after you graduate, leave school or drop below half-time enrollment.

## Question 3: How would I make repayments?

All at once? Nope. Here are some details about federal student loans: The "standard repayment" length is ten years. Repayment can happen faster or slower than ten years. It's entirely up to you (and depends on your career and income).

You can pay your bill online or by mail each month after your grace period ends. If you borrow $30,000 over four years (nearly the average), your monthly payment will be a little more than $300, depending on interest rates.

You can apply for a different repayment plan if you can't afford your monthly payment. In certain circumstances, you can even have the amount you owe forgiven.[41]

## Question 4: Will I be in debt for the rest of my life?

Not as long as you pay back what you owe on time.

And *how* do you do that?

### You get a job.

And *how* do you get a job with enough income to pay your debt?

### You graduate with a college degree.

If you need to give these questions more thought, it might be a good time to revisit the Loan Default Rates and Graduation Rates discussed in Chapter 3. When it comes to student loans, you need to understand what you'll be saying yes or no to – let's take a more in-depth look.

---

[40] For most students, federal student loans are the **only** loans they should ever consider.

[41] Loan forgiveness means that the government says, "You're off the hook for the money you owe us."

## Question 5: How do I get student loans, and where do they come from?

To receive federal student loans, you must:

1. Fill out the FAFSA, an application we'll cover in the next chapter.

2. When you receive college acceptance letters in the winter or spring, you'll also receive financial aid award letters. These letters will likely list some combination of grants, scholarships, work-study, and federal loans.

When you receive a financial aid award letter, you'll select the aid you want and leave what you don't. You don't have to take any loans if you don't want them, and you can accept less money than the amount offered. **Only borrow what you need.**

As a general guideline, the Consumer Financial Protection Bureau recommends not borrowing more (in total) than your expected annual salary after graduation. So, if you expect to make $50,000 in an entry-level job based on your career interests, don't borrow more than $50,000 while attending college.[42]

If you feel your net price for college is too high and the costs outweigh the benefits, don't feel obligated to take out loans. Look into your other options (hopefully, you applied to more than a few schools) and think about what is best for you in the long run.

## Question 6: What are the benefits and costs?

Most adults have debt in some form, and just like anything else, some manage it well, and some don't. If you have a particular type of debt (e.g., credit card debt) and you handle it poorly, you could be in severe, long-term financial trouble. Typically, this is because your credit card interest rate (the cost of borrowing) is likely to be high, and the goods/services you purchased with the debt are likely to have been consumed (e.g., food, going out, vacations, etc.) or depreciated (e.g., clothes, jewelry, etc.).

Think about the difference between taking out a student loan and buying some new clothes with your credit card. One will help you graduate on time so

---

[42] https://www.consumerfinance.gov/ask-cfpb/how-much-should-i-borrow-in-student-loans-en-579/

you can find a career and make more money long into the future. The other will become worn out and replaceable within a few years.

# *You don't want to be in debt for something that no longer provides you any benefit!*

If you carefully consider these five questions and exercise some self-control before deciding to borrow, it's possible to use debt to your advantage.

1. What type of asset am I purchasing? (e.g., a college education, a car, a home, new clothes, entertainment, etc.)

2. What are the benefits I'll receive from this asset? (e.g., personal achievement or success, higher future income, status, entertainment, etc.)

3. How long will these benefits last? (e.g., one day, month, year, entire life, etc.)

4. How much will it cost me to borrow the money I need?

5. When and how will I repay my debt? (e.g., payment of $280 once a month for four years)

Simply put, it can be wise to borrow money <u>when the benefits outweigh the costs</u>.

Benefits include access to goods (like a house) or services (like a college education). You want these benefits — financial, social, physical, etc. — to **last a long time** and **become more valuable** as time goes on.

**Costs** include an obligation to repay the money on time, with interest.

What are the benefits and costs of attending college?

| College | |
|---|---|
| Benefits and How Long They'll Last | Costs and How Long They'll Last |
| | |

Thought Box: Summarize answers to the 6 **BOLD** questions above...

#1: Why student debt can be useful?




#2: When will I repay?

Summary continued...

#3: How will I repay?

#4: Is it lifelong?

#5: How do I get approved for a student loan?

#6: Student loan costs and benefits...

---

### Intro to Interest: Brought to You by Hosna

Hosna borrows $20 from her bank for one year, agreeing to pay 10% interest. The agreement she made with her bank is called a **loan**. When it comes time to repay her loan, Hosna will pay back the $20, plus 10% of $20 — a total of $22.

The End.

The most important aspects of a loan are the following:

- **Principal**: The amount of money you borrow. In the story above: $20.

- **Interest Rate**: The interest rate is the cost of borrowing money, expressed as a percentage of your principal. In the story above, it is 10%.

- **Interest**: Interest is your cost to borrow money (in dollars). Calculate your interest by multiplying the principal by the interest rate. In Hosna's story: ($20 x 0.10) = $2.

**Since the interest rate represents *your borrowing cost*, you want it to be *as low as possible*.**

In real life, an interest rate can be:

- **fixed**, which means it doesn't change during the life of the loan[43], or

- **variable**, meaning the interest will change over time.

Variable rates may seem attractive if they're lower (initially) when compared to fixed rates, but they can be dangerous because of the unpredictability of the future. Along with other economic factors, interest rates change over time. You might be super excited when the bank offers you an initial variable rate of 4%, but within a year, you could be paying 5% and then 8% a few years after that, and so on.

Choose fixed-rate loans if you want to take on less risk, even if the interest is slightly higher than variable-rate loans. Think about the peace of mind you get by locking in a certain rate (and payment) for the entire life of the loan, which could be ten years or longer.

If you know your borrowing costs from the beginning, there's less risk from the future unknown.

Now, let's look at some real student loans and compare their interest rates.[44]

---

[43] The "life" of a loan refers to the length of time the money is borrowed.
[44] As of October 2024. https://studentaid.gov/understand-aid/types/loans/interest-rates

# Interest Rate Table

| Rank | Name | Lender | Interest Rate |
|------|------|--------|---------------|
| 1. | Direct Subsidized Loan | U.S. Gov't. | 6.53% (fixed) |
| 2. | Direct Unsubsidized Loan | U.S. Gov't. | 6.53% (fixed) |
| 3. | Direct PLUS Loan | U.S. Gov't. | 9.08% (fixed) |
| 4. | Private Student Loan | Bank | 3% – 18% (fixed or variable) |

## Student Loans Compared to Other Loans

Does borrowing for your education cost more or less than borrowing for other things? To answer this question, let's compare interest rates on student loans to interest rates on other popular loans. These are the average interest rates as of October 2024.

| Loan (Asset) | Annual Percentage Rate (APR) |
|--------------|------------------------------|
| Federal Student Loan (Education) | 6.53% |
| Auto Loan (Car) | 6.84% (new)and 12.01% (used) |
| Mortgage, 30-year fixed (House) | 6.18% |
| Credit Card (Any Purchase) | 22.76% |
| Pay Day Loan (Any Purchase) | 400% |

Thought Box:

79

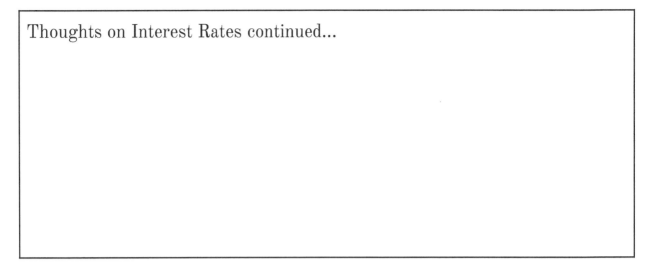

Thoughts on Interest Rates continued...

The cost of borrowing money for your education looks pretty good compared to borrowing for other purchases, right? Let's take a quick look at one additional cost of borrowing money.

## Loan Fees

Federal loans and many private loans have loan fees, charged as a percentage (1.057% currently, for federal loans) of the principal.

Loan fees work like this: if you take a $5,000 Direct Unsubsidized Loan from the federal government, you will receive $52.85 *less* than $5,000, which is $4,946.70. The $52.85 fee is 1.057% of $5,000. Heads up – Direct PLUS loans have a much higher fee of 4.228%.

In a perfect world, you'd rather not pay interest or fees. But, if a few thousand dollars is the only thing between you and your college degree, the benefits of taking out a loan will likely outweigh its costs in the long run.

## Federal vs. Private

I'm just going to repeat it very clearly: **federal student loans are better than private student loans.** Here's why:

1. They cost you less. Federal loans will almost certainly have lower interest rates than private loans.

2. They have a fixed rate. With federal student loans, you don't have to

worry about your interest rate changing at any time.

3. Your credit score is *not* taken into account for federal student loans (except for PLUS loans) — meaning you can borrow if you have no credit history at all, which is the case for many high school students.

4. Some federal loans are **subsidized**, meaning the U.S. government pays the interest on the loan while you're still enrolled in school. These loans are awesome because *you get to borrow this money for free* until you graduate.[45]

5. Direct Subsidized Loans and Federal Perkins Loans are need-based. You'll qualify for them if you demonstrate financial need on the FAFSA, which means you don't have to go through a separate application process.

6. Most federal loans have a grace period, giving you time to transition out of college and settle into a new home, job, and budget before you start paying the loans back. Some private loans have grace periods, but some don't.

7. Federal loans allow you to choose from a variety of repayment plans. You can choose a plan with lower monthly payments based on your income, or even get your loans forgiven.

8. If you're struggling financially, you'd rather have federal than private loans. The federal government is flexible with students, allowing you to qualify for a deferment (postponing your payments without defaulting).

Here's a quick example of when I qualified for deferment: A few years after graduating from college, I volunteered in Micronesia, earning a stipend of $300 per month. I couldn't afford my $175 monthly student loan payment during this time, so I contacted my federal loan provider, and they placed my loans in deferment. There was no penalty, and the process was easy. I was just asked to update them on my work status the following year.

Read more about deferment here at the studentaid.ed.gov website.

---

[45] Or drop below half-time enrollment.

# Timeline:

## Before Borrowing

Before taking out loans, you need to be confident that you'll graduate from college with a job and a lifestyle where you **earn more money than you spend**.

| Careers I'm Considering | Starting Salaries (in the state you want to live) |
| --- | --- |
|  |  |
|  |  |
|  |  |

Just because you *can* borrow money doesn't mean you *should*. You shouldn't borrow $80,000 for college unless you're comfortable paying over $800 monthly after graduation.

Estimate your future salary, then calculate your monthly income after taxes using the ADP Paycheck Calculator (Google it, or go here: https://www.adp.com/resources/tools/calculators/states/california-salary-paycheck-calculator.aspx

| Career | Potential Salary | Monthly Income after Tax |
| --- | --- | --- |
|  | $ | $ |
|  | $ | $ |
|  | $ | $ |

1. Based on your work with Net Price Calculators in the previous chapter, how much in student loans do you think you'll need each year?

2. What is the total amount you'll need to borrow to graduate?

3. Take 1% of your total amount borrowed to find your approximate monthly payment after graduation:

4. Is your monthly payment affordable, given your future salary?

## *While Borrowing*

You won't need to pay for your student loans while you're still enrolled in school at least half-time. For now, focus on managing your path toward graduation, attending class, and not overspending. In your last two years of college, you should start thinking about possible careers, apply for a summer internship to build your experience, and check out a campus job fair to connect with employers.

If you're planning to do something non-traditional — maybe you decide to volunteer in the Peace Corps or work for Teach for America — plan out the process for deferring your loans or choosing the best repayment plan, and check your options for forgiveness. Contact your school's financial aid office or call your loan provider if you have questions.

## *After Borrowing*

With your new income and expenses, you should work on balancing your budget during your six-month grace period. Then, set up autopay to make it easy to make on-time payments from your checking account.

**BONUS**: If you choose to set up autopay for your federal loans, you'll even get a nice little bonus: a 0.25% interest rate reduction. You can usually set up autopay by following the instructions on your first bill or by calling your lender directly. The alternative is to write a check every month.

### PSLF

Another way to eliminate student loans is to enroll in Public Service Loan Forgiveness (PSLF). If you work in public service (as a teacher, firefighter, police officer, etc.), with a non-profit organization (Greenpeace, UNICEF, etc.), or as a volunteer (with AmeriCorps or the Peace Corps), you can get some or all of your loans forgiven.

Only Federal Direct Loans are eligible for PSLF. Loan forgiveness can be tricky, so do some research before committing to PSLF. Be strategic and proactive if you want to benefit from PSLF. Read more about loan forgiveness here: https://studentaid.gov/manage-loans/forgiveness-cancellation.

## Tax Benefits?

Yes, please! The U.S. government provides tax benefits for your federal and private student loan expenses because they want you to get your education. When you pay interest on your student loans, you reduce the amount of taxes you have to pay that year (this is called your **tax liability**). The more you reduce your tax liability, the less taxes you owe!

To check out the tax benefits of student loans in detail, go to:

https://www.irs.gov/newsroom/tax-benefits-for-education-information-center

## Heads Up!

*"Lower your rate!!!"* I still get emails and letters like this every month, and they go straight to the trash. Be cautious when a company sends "official" looking mail with an urgent request for you to allow them to help lower your rate, manage your debt for you, forgive your debt, or consolidate your loans. Most likely, they'll hit you up while you're paying off your loans after college.

Remember, these companies are trying to make money from you, and some are outright scams. You may save money in the short term, but it could cost you more in the long term.

## CHAPTER RECAP

1. Before borrowing money, carefully weigh the costs and benefits of your investment, confidently understand the terms of the loan, and be prepared to repay the money on time and in full.

2. Choose fixed, low-interest rate loans if you need to borrow to pay for college.

3. The federal government offers the best loans. Most of them are available without any credit history; you just need to fill out the FAFSA.

4. If you see loans offered in your financial aid award letter, don't accept

them unless you need them.

5. Plan to have a job and a lifestyle where you earn more money than you spend.

Here are some general guidelines to follow when looking at your financial aid award letter:

1. The grants and scholarships are free money, so obviously, you want those. Make sure you understand any obligations on your end of the deal — many scholarships require you to maintain a certain GPA in college.

2. Take advantage of work-study if it's offered in your financial aid package. It'll be nice to have extra income from an on-campus job where you work flexible hours depending on your class schedule.

3. Loans should be the last form of financial aid you receive because you have to pay this money back, plus interest. Again, don't accept this money unless you *need* it. And if you take a student loan, make sure you know what your monthly payment will eventually be.

Blank Space Just For You

# FAFSA and the CSS Profile

Okay, timeout. Before we get to your pre-chapter thoughts, most of this book has been about uncovering the right way to do things, but let's take a break to look at some bad financial and educational decisions.

---

Here's a little story about Stu. Stu went to nearby Crasto College, which costs $10,000 per year. Stu thought he was getting a good deal compared to what he might pay at other universities.

Stu did not realize, however, that Crasto had just a 25% graduation rate and a 30% loan default rate. These rates mean only one in four students received a degree from Crasto, and about one in three were in severe financial trouble after graduation. Despite Crasto's "cheap" price tag, the odds were actually against Stu from the start.

Stu applied for financial aid by filling out the FAFSA – his one good move – and received a grant for $5,000 for his first year at Crasto. Unfortunately, he forgot to resubmit the FAFSA during his freshman year and didn't receive any more aid for his sophomore year. Stu often joked about his procrastination, though truthfully, he knew his jokes weren't funny.

Stu's G.P.A. started dropping. Unlike his high school, Crasto College never contacted him or his parents to discuss his troubles. It wasn't their problem. Stu ended up quitting school because he wanted to "focus on other priorities." He had a serious girlfriend and wanted to increase his hours at a part-time job to increase his income.

However, Stu's restaurant couldn't give him any more hours. They eventually fired him because he was more interested in playing video games on his phone than serving customers.

Sadly, Stu lost his job just as his student loan payments began coming due. (Since he had completely stopped taking classes, he now needed to start paying down his debt.) Without his job, Stu could not pay his $75 monthly loan and defaulted. Default severely damaged Stu's credit history, and now no landlord will rent him an apartment. Stu moved back to his parent's house and currently shares a room with his younger brother. Stu feels like his luck has run out.

You can avoid Stu's fate. Take your college goals seriously, find the support you need to succeed, and take action to receive the financial aid you need.

---

Pre-Chapter Thoughts:

1. What did Stu do (and not do) to end up in a troubled situation? What mindset do you need to avoid ending up like Stu?

2. You've got to do some work to get financial aid. How much time and effort are you willing to put into making college affordable for you?

3. Do you know anyone who has received a scholarship? What do you know about the organization that gave them the money? How much money did they receive?

*We have focused so much on how to get into college, but everyone seems to overlook how important it is for us to learn how to pay for our education. There are so many misconceptions out there about the cost of college, and this project helped me understand the truth. - Ellie H.*

## The FAFSA.

## WHAT?

You've heard the name, but what exactly is it? It's the Free Application for Federal Student Aid. So, the FAFSA is free. It's an application (it takes you less than an hour to fill out online).

## WHY?

You complete the FAFSA to receive financial aid - grants, work-study, loans - from the federal government, state government, and universities to pay for the costs of college. The FAFSA is the main form[46] you'll use to prove you *need* financial aid.

Your requirement to show proof makes sense — this aid is intended to go *to students who genuinely need it* to pay for higher education. Every year, this application provides the gateway to <u>billions of dollars</u> in financial aid for millions of students at thousands of colleges.

## WHEN?

You'll submit the FAFSA in 12th grade. These past few years have been a mess with the FAFSA (it's being redesigned). In 2024, the FAFSA will be available on December 1st for students attending college in the 2025-26 school year. Normally, the FAFSA is available on October 1 each year.

You'll need to submit a new FAFSA before each year of college. You won't need to fill it out your senior year of college unless you're planning on continuing your education past your 4th year.

---

[46] Others include the CSS Profile and California Dream Act Application.

# HOW?

When you fill out the FAFSA, take time to complete it correctly. Make sure to accurately input personal information, including your name, social security number, and family income level.

**Q:** *What if I have a social security number, but my parents don't?*

**A:** Input your social security number and then enter all zeros (000-00-0000) for parents or guardians who don't have one.[2] *Do not* just make up a number. Parents without an SSN will need to print, sign, and mail the signature page instead of using the FAFSA online signature.

**Q:** *What if I don't have a social security number?*

**A:** If you don't have a social security number, you won't be filling out the FAFSA, but you still might have great options for financial aid. One of these options could be the CSS Profile, which we'll discuss near the end of this chapter.

If you live in California, your best option to receive significant financial aid is the CA Dream Act Application — we'll cover this in the next chapter!

When filling out the FAFSA, have the following information (from you **and** your parents/guardians) available:

- Social Security Numbers

- Birth Dates

- Driver's License (if any)

- Tax Returns for the previous year (if any)

- W-2 Form (your employer sends you this, usually in January of each year, to communicate your income and taxes for the previous year)

- Any other info related to assets (money or things of value), extra income, or investments (if you or your parents had any)

- FSA ID for both you and one parent or guardian (I'll explain this soon)

**NOTE:** Except for the CSS Profile, applying for financial aid is *free*. Some shady companies try to charge you fees for help on the FAFSA. Avoid them. As a high school student, you are very capable of filling out the FAFSA. Seek advice from your high school counselor, studentaid.gov, and fafsa.gov.

## STEPS TO COMPLETE

### Before October 1st (12th Grade):

1. Get familiar with the FAFSA. Look at the Federal Student Aid website or YouTube channel for tutorials.

2. Create your personal Federal Student Aid ID (FSA ID) at the studentaid.gov website. If you are a dependent,[47] one of your parents will also need to create a separate FSA ID for her or himself.

   These FSA IDs will allow both of you to access and sign the FAFSA electronically.

3. If you want to get a quick estimate of how much federal student aid you might receive, go here: https://studentaid.gov/aid-estimator/

### What to Do After October 1st:

1. It's game time. Go to https://studentaid.gov/ and select the link to apply for aid using the FAFSA form.

2. Avoid common FAFSA mistakes! Learn more here:

   https://www.nasfaa.org/fafsa_tips

---

[47] You're a dependent if you live with your parents/guardians, you're under 24 years old, and don't have any children.

3. If your parents are divorced, separated, remarried, or unable to submit their information due to special circumstances, please determine whose information to use on the FAFSA by going to:

https://studentaid.gov/apply-for-aid/fafsa/filling-out/parent-info

4. When filling out the FAFSA online, you'll be able to list up to 20 universities you want to receive your financial information. Add these colleges even if you haven't applied (yet).

5. Once you submit your FAFSA, you'll see the status of your application as "Processed." You'll get a confirmation that shows your estimated "SAI" or Student Aid Index. The SAI is used by colleges to determine your eligibility for financial aid.

6. After your FAFSA is processed, you'll receive your "FAFSA Submission Summary." Look it over to make sure all the information looks accurate. NOTE: It won't tell you how much financial aid you'll receive – for that, you'll need to wait until you get your Financial Aid Award Letters from colleges that have admitted you.

7. To help you make the most sense of your financial aid award letter, check out this webinar:

https://bigfuture.collegeboard.org/for-parents/webinar-comparing-financial-aid-awards

## THE CSS PROFILE

Hundreds of colleges and scholarship providers use the College Scholarship Service (CSS) Profile to determine your eligibility for financial aid. The CSS Profile asks questions similar to those on the FAFSA, but it's a little more detailed in regards to your family's finances. The College Board website says that the form usually takes between 45 minutes and 2 hours to complete.

The CSS Profile costs $25 and is offered online by The College Board (the same organization that offers the SAT and AP Tests). If your family income is $100,000 or less, you've qualified for an SAT fee waiver, or you're an orphan or ward of the court, you can get a fee waiver, meaning you won't have to pay the $25 fee.

You do *not* need to fill out the CSS Profile unless it's required by one of the colleges you're applying to. To see a list of the colleges that use the CSS Profile, visit https://www.collegeboard.org/profilelist. Be sure to look up each school's deadline for the CSS Profile — either check online or give the financial aid office a call. Find out if your focus schools require you to fill out the CSS Profile, and if so, write their submission deadlines below.

| Focus Schools | CSS Deadline? |
|---|---|
| (Safety) | |
| (Match) | |
| (Reach) | |

Remember, if you submit the CSS Profile, you still need to fill out the FAFSA. To read more about the CSS Profile and fill out the application, go to http://css.collegeboard.org.

### FAFSA & CSS IMPORTANT FACTS

| | FAFSA | CSS Profile |
|---|---|---|
| Date Available | October 1 | October 1 |
| Cost | Free | $25 |
| Completion Required? | Yes[48] | If your college or scholarship provider requires it |
| Submission Deadline | Early March of your Senior Year | Varies by college |
| Website | https://studentaid.gov/ | http://css.collegeboard.org |

---

[48] Unless you're undocumented – then you'll complete the CA Dream ACT Application and CSS Profile (if needed)

# WE "MAKE TOO MUCH"

Before receiving your financial aid offer, it's important to set realistic expectations. Based on your results from net price calculators, you may realize your family's financial situation will prevent you from getting the financial aid you want.

And for those who are offered "a lot" of financial aid, it's still fairly common for the aid amount to be less than what is needed to cover all the costs. If you're concerned about high net prices, be proactive and explore the following options.

**Option #1 (before receiving your award letter):** *Regardless of your financial situation*, fill out the FAFSA, even if you think your family makes too much to qualify for any need-based financial aid. You have nothing to lose. Also, apply to colleges that request the CSS Profile. This application requires financial aid applicants to submit more information (e.g., the cost of living) compared to the FAFSA. The CSS Profile will possibly help you demonstrate that you have a higher need than it may seem on the FAFSA.

**Option #2 (before receiving your award letter):** Apply for more scholarships!

**Option #3 (before and after receiving your award letter):** Get a part-time job to help you pay your way.

**Option #4 (before and after receiving your award letter):** Talk to the college's financial aid office. Let them know your situation and see if there's anything they can recommend. If you've already received your award letter and it's not enough, try using this link as a guide to negotiate a better financial aid package: https://www.cnn.com/2023/04/28/business/college-financial-aid/index.html

**Option #5 (after receiving your award letter):** Make a "Professional Judgment Appeal." This option is a little more official than Option #4. If your family's financial status recently changed, or you feel that you have circumstances beyond your control that prevent you from contributing the amount calculated by the FAFSA, you can make a "Professional Judgment

96

Appeal" to the college's financial aid administrator.

Financial aid administrators are allowed to change aid awards on a case-by-case basis after they review these appeals. You might also help your case if you're able to show a better financial aid package offered to you by another similarly competitive college.

Remember to be considerate, professional, and polite in your communication with the financial aid office staff. They weren't the ones who put you in your current financial situation, so don't blame them. If there's something they can do to help, they will do it.

**Option #6 (before and after receiving your award letter):** Review other options in Chapters 4 and 6 (loans).

**Option #7 (after receiving your award letter):** Choose another school.

## CHAPTER RECAP

1. The FAFSA is possibly the **most important** part of your entire financial aid journey.

2. Fill out the FAFSA. https://studentaid.gov/

3. Fill out the FAFSA. It's available October 1st (delayed in 2023 and 2024).

4. Fill out the FAFSA. It should take less than an hour.

5. Fill out the FAFSA. Call a college's financial aid office or ask your high school counselor if you need help.

6. Fill out the FAFSA. Complete it every October before your next year of college.

7. Fill out the CSS Profile if required by any universities you're applying to.

8. Don't be like Stu.

Blank Space Just For You

# 8

# A DREAM Come True

- **If you and your parents have social security numbers, you can skip this chapter because you'll fill out the FAFSA.**

- **If you have a social security number but your parents are undocumented, you can also skip this chapter since you can still submit the FAFSA.**

- **If you don't have a social security number, this chapter is for you — please read on!**

Pre-Chapter Thoughts:

1. What are some challenges you've faced as an undocumented student? How did you overcome them? Who has helped you along the way?

_____

_____

_____

_____

_____

_____

2. What future challenges might you face? What resources (including people) are available to help you overcome these challenges?

_____

_____

_____

_____

_____

3. Who inspires you? Who do you wish to inspire?

_____

_____

_____

_____

_____

_____

*This project has definitely lifted that weight off my shoulders. I know beyond a shadow of a doubt that I will attend college and nothing is going to stop me. I will always look back on this project when I am applying to college. This project has been beyond helpful. - Lauren T.*

## CHAPTER UPDATE

As an undocumented student, you may feel overwhelmed by the additional challenges of making college happen without a social security number. Stress from these challenges has become magnified since the original publication of this book, as dreamers' opportunities have been subject to significant and unpredictable change.

To get the latest updates and resources, go to the primary Dream Act Site: https://www.csac.ca.gov/cadaa-resources, and follow the links included below.

Now, let's get started.

## THE LAWS

Two governments affect each student's journey to college: the U.S. (or federal) government and the state government. Here are some key facts related to their laws:

- First, you *don't* have to be an American citizen to attend college in the United States.

- Without U.S. citizenship, you do not qualify for federal financial aid. However, you might be eligible for state financial aid and lower in-state tuition prices.

Even though the laws in the U.S. don't prevent undocumented students from attending college, the decision to provide access is passed on to each college. For public colleges (think community colleges, Cal States, UCs), this means it's the state's decision.

The good news is that most colleges — especially those in California — don't require proof of citizenship or immigration status to apply. It is also important to note that the CA Dream Act is **not related** to DACA. This is good news for dreamers living in California.

## PROFESSIONAL ADVICE AND RESOURCES

When looking for additional help, pick up the phone and call the financial aid office or the undocumented student services office at any college! I called the Undocumented Student Service Offices at both UCLA and UCSC for help writing this chapter, and they were super helpful. If you're looking for help online, remember to investigate the credibility of each source you find.

**DO NOT pay for advice or access to scholarships!** One great app that helps undocumented students find scholarships is called DREAMer's RoadMap (Google it). For additional help, here are some credible websites to help you find the guidance you may be looking for:

### Government Resources

- CA Dream Act Info and link to Application:

https://dream.csac.ca.gov/

- Q&A on Federal Student Aid for undocumented students:

https://studentaid.gov/apply-for-aid/fafsa/filling-out/undocumented-students

### California University Resources

- UC Dream Act Support: https://undoc.universityofcalifornia.edu/

- CA Community College Support:

https://www.cccco.edu/Students/Support-Services/Special-population/Undocumented-Students

## Community Resources

- Support for immigrant youth: https://immigrantsrising.org/

- Legal Support: http://www.maldef.org/

- Online community for first-generation college students:

  http://www.imfirst.org/

- Scholarship Search for Undocumented Students:

  https://www.dreamersroadmap.com/

Find three to four scholarships available to you as a dreamer.

| Scholarship Name | Description and $ Amount | Application Deadline |
|---|---|---|
|  |  |  |
|  |  |  |
|  |  |  |
|  |  |  |

- 6 Things Undocumented Students Need to Know About College (from the College Board):

https://bigfuture.collegeboard.org/plan-for-college/get-started/6-things-undocumented-students-need-to-know-about-college

- The DREAM.US scholarship: http://www.thedream.us/
- General information and resources for undocumented immigrants: https://mydocumentedlife.org/

### THE STORIES OF CHRISTHIAN AND FABIOLA

There are many encouraging stories of dreamers succeeding in college. The video — "UC Berkeley's Undocumented Student Program: Your Campus, Your Community" — shares the stories of a few students, including Christhian and Fabiola, as they journey through college. Google it or type in the link below.
https://www.youtube.com/watch?v=L18atoZUbOw

### CHAPTER RECAP

1. It's possible to receive financial support from the state of California and your university (but not the federal government) if you are undocumented.

2. In the changing political climate, be sure to contact the undocumented student programs at different universities. They're a great resource to help with any questions, even if you're not going to attend the university you contact.

3. Gather the information necessary to fill out the CA Dream Act Application and go for it!

Blank Space Just For You...

# 9

# The Summary

Pre-Chapter Thoughts:

1. Were you open to changing your mind throughout this project? How have your ideas about paying for college and attending college changed?

_____

_____

_____

_____

_____

2. What have you done up to this point to help prepare for your future?

_____

_____

_____

_____

*I was worried this whole Junior year, whether I was doing enough to get into college and how I would be able to afford it. I can truly say I was stressed about college. But the recent project not only relieved my stress, it also gave me very important information that I can now use when applying to college. - Daniel C.*

# I

Congrats on finishing Part I of your college research adventure! I hope you've found some clarity as you complete this journey and begin another one. This chapter includes some key points you've heard throughout this book, along with a quick summary. Part II ahead will dive deeper into additional college-related topics.

If you're interested in attending a particular college, now is the time! Fill out the FAFSA and apply for additional scholarships. Wait for your financial aid award letter (after you're admitted) to figure out if you can afford to attend.

Before you make the final decision to accept or decline your admission, get answers to any questions you have about financial aid. Call the college's financial aid office, and ask them anything!

College is worth the investment of your time and money as long as you:
- Graduate
- Get a job that pays you for your college education.

Don't let your future job or your major put you in a box. Things change, and that's ok. Your college degree (regardless of major) should provide you with more flexibility to handle the changes. College degrees have value even if you're not sure what career path you want.

Focus on attending a college with the academic, social, and geographical environment that will support you in your goal of graduating.

## II

Use the College Scorecard or College Navigator to research average net prices, graduation rates, and loan default rates of colleges you'd like to attend. These statistics help paint a picture of the *real cost* of attendance and whether or not students are accomplishing their goals at each college.

Consider both need-based and merit-based aid when calculating your cost. Federal and state aid are available, and many colleges are also huge providers of financial aid every year. Revisit Chapter 4 for a refresher. Estimate your personal cost of college by using Net Price Calculators. Look for additional scholarships, part-time work, and student loans to help cover the remaining costs to attend your college of choice.

Federal student loans (especially subsidized loans) can provide you with a low-cost way to pay for part of college. Consider using loans if:

- the benefits of a college degree outweigh your borrowing costs and
- you're confident in your ability to stick with the college until you graduate.

Don't borrow money unless it's necessary and you understand when/how you'll pay your loan off.

## III

The FAFSA is your gateway to most of the financial aid available. Depending on the colleges you're applying to, you may also need to submit the CSS Profile to receive financial aid from specific universities.

You may still qualify for financial aid by submitting the CA Dream Act Application if you cannot complete the FAFSA due to your citizenship status. Whatever situation you're in, you have financial aid options.

When you receive financial aid award letters, you can choose what money to accept or decline. Not all financial aid is created equal, and you do NOT have to accept all the aid offered. Here is the order in which you should accept financial aid:

1. **Grants and Scholarships** — Gotta love free money!

2. **Work-study** — This is an opportunity to get a flexible job (on or near campus). Your paychecks go straight to your pocket, so you can spend the money on anything you'd like.

3. **Federal student loans** — Federal loans (both subsidized and unsubsidized) allow access to college at low interest rates with flexible repayment plans. *Subsidized loans* should always be selected before unsubsidized loans since you won't have to pay interest while in school.

4. **Private loans** — Avoid them unless absolutely necessary! Private loans often charge the most interest and are the least flexible in repayment.

Blank Space Just For You...

# PART II

# DEEPER DIVES

"Success is the sum of small efforts, repeated day-in and day-out." - Robert Collier

# Part A

# Glossary of College Words

## KEY TERMS PART I: WHO ARE YOU?

- If you're taking classes to get a bachelor's degree or associate's degree in college, you'll be known as an **undergraduate student** or "undergrad" for short.

- A **bachelor's degree** is awarded to students who complete course requirements at a four-year college or university.

- An **associate's degree** is awarded to students who complete course requirements at a two-year community college.

A bachelor's degree might take more or less than four years to complete, and an associate's degree might take more or less than two years to complete - it just depends on the classes you take and the credits you earn.

As an undergrad, your cost of attendance includes three big expenses (tuition, room, and board) and many smaller ones (fees, books, supplies, health insurance, etc.).

- **Tuition** - the money you pay to enroll in classes.

- **Room** - the cost of your housing or dorm.

- **Board** - the cost of food. At many universities, first-year students have a meal plan that includes pre-paid food they can get on campus.

*Most college students use _financial aid_ to help pay for the cost of attendance.*

- **Financial Aid** - money (in the form of grants, scholarships, income from a job, loans) offered to students to help pay for college.

# KEY TERMS PART II: WHAT IS COLLEGE?

- Four-year **colleges** and **universities** technically have some differences[49], but when I use these terms throughout this book, I'm talking about the same thing: a school where you get a *bachelor's degree*.

- When I refer specifically to a **community college** in this book, I'm talking about a two-year education that leads to an *associate's degree* or a transfer to a four-year college.

*Colleges are either "Public" or "Private."*

- **Public** colleges receive funding from the state government and student tuition. They usually offer lower tuition rates to students who are residents.[50]

- **Private** colleges don't receive funding from the state, so they rely on tuition and private donations.

- For now, it's important to know that the public and private schools I reference in the main chapters of this book are **non-profit**. There are also **private for-profit schools**, which are discussed briefly in the "Extras."

## Different "types" of Colleges:[51]

- **Arts** colleges focus on training students in the arts.

- **Vocational and Technical** colleges focus on training students for specific careers.

- **Liberal Arts** colleges focus broadly on the humanities and sciences.

- **Single-sex** colleges are specifically men-only or women-only.

- **Religious** colleges, where students may or may not have religious course requirements.

- **MSIs** (Minority-serving Institutions) include:

---

[49] Differences include size (some universities contain many colleges within them), degrees offered (some colleges only offer undergraduate degrees), and educational focus (research universities, for example).
[50] Residents are people who live in the state.
[51] Many of these terms are paraphrased from
https://bigfuture.collegeboard.org/find-colleges/college-101/types-of-colleges-the-basics

○ **HBCUs** (Historically Black Colleges and Universities) that focus on educating African-American students.

○ **HSIs** (Hispanic-serving Institutions) that focus on educating Hispanic students, where at least 25% of their student population is Hispanic.[52]

---

[52] All colleges accept students of all races, to be clear.

# Part B
# How to Succeed in College

"I wanted to leave halfway through my first year. I thought everyone was smarter than me, and I always felt more comfortable at home with family and my high school friends.

"But I began to have small successes here and there – a friendly encounter, an above-average grade on a quiz, a discussion where somebody valued my question or statement. These successes started to build on one another over time, and I felt like a member of my college community.

"I realized I did belong there.

"Honestly, I don't think I would have grown into who I am today if it wasn't as hard as it was for me. I was learning not just about new concepts in my classes but about who I was and what I wanted to do with my life."

- Anonymous.

---

Watch this!

Khan Academy has many brief video interviews about applying to college, paying for college, and overcoming challenges in college!

Use Google to find them

---

**On Struggle:** College struggles are a reality for every student. If you understand the benefits of struggle and believe you can grow from mistakes, you can succeed in college.

Every person will struggle as they put effort towards something they value. You just need to decide whether you are willing to have college be that "something" for a few years.

**Why do some students drop out?** A research study funded by the Bill and Melinda Gates Foundation, "With Their Whole Lives Ahead of Them," set out to find differences between students who graduate and those who drop out. Of those who dropped out:

- More than half of the students said, "Needing to work and make money" was a major reason for dropping out.

- About 6 in 10 said they didn't have financial support from their parents.

- About 7 in 10 said they didn't have financial aid, such as loans or scholarships.

What does this mean for the difference between those who graduate and those who drop out? It's not about whether or not you can understand the content in your classes, your major, or your G.P.A. in high school. **It's about balancing your work, school, and family responsibilities.**

It's about understanding your financial situation and opportunity costs associated with work and school. It's about getting help when you need it. When you've got uncertainty in your life, the following can make all the difference:

1. Advocate for yourself and ask for guidance. You won't know everything, and that's okay.

2. Call your financial aid office to get help paying for college (which includes paying for your housing and your food).

3. Try to attend school full-time so that you can graduate on time. Every year added to the normal graduation time (two or four years) is another year without earning a full-time college grad salary, which on average totals $500 more per week. Sometimes, it's worth it to take out a loan instead of working the extra hours. Consider the sacrifices you can make today to benefit yourself in the future.

4. Make sure you're taking the classes you *need* to get your degree.

5. Refocus and rest - self-care is essential. What are three healthy ways

you deal with stress? (Some ideas might include running, hiking, playing sports, listening to music, playing music, dancing, gaming, reading, journaling, praying, meditating, playing card games, building something, talking to a friend or family member, learning something new, etc.)

My Thoughts:

1.

2.

3.

Know that you are not alone in the challenges you face. Try to find a mentor to help you through it. Ask a former teacher to lunch, set up a meeting with your adviser/counselor, or find an older friend who has graduated.

# Part C

# Online vs. In-Person

Choosing the "right learning environment" in the 21st century also usually includes weighing the decision to take one or more classes online. Since you'll likely be given this option in college, it's worth looking into the pros and cons of learning online.

### What Makes Online Classes Good

- They allow you to learn from the convenience of your home.

- They give you access to any subject you're interested in at any time.

### What Makes Online Classes Tough

- You need great focus to learn anything in an online course. I'm not talking about a 10-minute Khan Academy video but a full-blown online class. Getting distracted while watching lectures or working on assignments online is incredibly easy. You'll have other websites competing for your attention and face distractions from other things in your surroundings.

  If you're taking courses from home, there might be other people around who want to talk, and you might get hungry in the middle of the lecture, and your pet might be nagging you for attention, all at the same time. In a classroom, you have more limited options - listen to the lecture, talk to a classmate, or sneak around on your phone.

- If you're in an online class, you usually miss out on the human aspect of learning. Sure, you have "discussions" where you have to create one thread and then post a reply to two others, but let's be honest: you (or most people, at least) will skim through the shortest thread and write the quickest reply possible for credit. It's not likely you'll ever revisit the thread to see if anyone (including the teacher) responded to your response, so any meaningful dialogue is rare.

- Classroom discussions are essential for many of us (even if you tend to be an introvert). Defending reasoning among peers, responding live in real-time, and using non-verbal communication allows students to push their thinking and process new ideas. You'll completely miss out on that when you're learning online.

I'm not arguing that online classes are worthless. But we must be honest with ourselves—online learning has specific challenges. If you just want to get a course out of the way or can't get to campus, grind out an online class.

But if you sincerely want to learn the concepts you're studying, you should strive to be present in the classroom and actively participate. For me and countless others, online courses just don't provide the same quality of educational experience as classroom courses.

My experience with online classes compared to in-person classes:

How my experience might be different with such classes in college:

# Part D

# Choosing a Major

## Diego's Experience

As a teenager, Diego struggled to understand what he was "good at." Diego knew he liked helping people with personal issues and trying new things. He often thought, "Why can't I just be great at music or football or something else that's obvious?"

At first, Diego thought he wanted to make a lot of money to buy a big house and a fancy car. He decided that being a doctor would be a good career since he could help people, too.

While in college, Diego realized he had a problem: he wasn't interested in his science classes. Thinking it wasn't worth it to work the rest of his life in a field that didn't genuinely interest him, Diego decided to go back to his roots and refocus his energy on helping people. If he got paid a lot of money for his work, cool, but if he couldn't cash in, that was all right, too. At the end of his sophomore year, Diego switched his major from Pre-Med (Biology) to Social Work.

---

For many careers, your choice of major is less important than your degree itself. Many students change majors at least once, so try to give yourself some slack if you don't get it right the first time. That said, we don't want to ignore this decision entirely. Consider the following questions for guidance on finding a starting point in choosing a major.

1.  What are you most curious about? Often, we're anxious because we haven't found a passion yet, or we limit our options to what we think we're "good at." But what you're good at when you're 17 is not necessarily what you'll be good at when you're 22. You were probably terrible at walking 16 years ago, but look at you now! When you think about choosing a major, go with something you genuinely want to learn more about.

2.  Is there anything you never want to study again? If you just can't stand another (fill in the blank) class for the rest of your life, ask a college counselor or do some online research to find the course

requirements for different majors.

3. Do you want to focus on skills from the "heart?" We often forget that we can be good at things that are not tangible - things we cannot see or touch. To find professional success in the 21st century, "soft skills" like the following are often essential:

- speaking and listening,

- creativity,

- problem-solving,

- maintaining relationships, and

- being an inspiring leader.

Some majors can help you develop all of these skills.

**Some help to get the ball rolling**

If you're not sure what field you might want to major in, try thinking about what activities in everyday life you enjoy. For example:

- Do you feel a greater sense of purpose when you help out those in need?

- Was it easy to stay up all night planning your family's Thanksgiving?

- Does time fly by when you're editing photos and posting them on Instagram?

- Did you get into a heated debate over who should have won that sports game?

- Do you feel valued when you help your friends through difficult times?

Based on your answers to these questions, you might be able to find a major that interests you in one of the fields on the next page.

| Love Music | Love Entertainment | Love Nature |
|---|---|---|
| Music Therapy, Iovine-Young Academy, Music Business, Jazz Studies | Film, Animation, Theater Arts, Game Design, Screenwriting, Graphic Design, Digital Media | Wildlife Conservation, Oceanography, Zoology, Agriculture, Biology, Botany, Environmental Science |

| Love People | Love Deep Thought | Love Food |
|---|---|---|
| Communication, Psychology, Education, Sociology, Political Science, Criminal Justice, Social Work | History, Linguistics, Cultural Studies, Philosophy, Cognitive Science, Religious Studies | Culinary Arts, Nutrition, Viticulture, Food Science, Dairy Science, Sustainable Agriculture |

Thought Box:

Many students choose a college and major because they want specific career options as an adult. In the next section, we'll take a quick look at careers.

# Part E

# Choosing a Career

## The Stories of Evan, Roxanne, and Steve

An 8-year-old kid named Evan created a million-dollar business just by opening presents on YouTube.

Artist and single mom Roxanne Quimby started making candles from unused bee's wax in Maine and, 23 years later, sold her empire, Burt's Bees, for $970 million.

Steve Ells wasn't the first person to sell tasty burritos, but from 1993 to 2016, he built Chipotle into a company worth more than $16 billion.

For these people, money came second to passion. They found out what sparked their curiosity and brought them joy, then figured out how to do it for a living. Thinking about what's possible for you five years from now is tough.

Consider how quickly our society (and our work) is changing. Just ten years ago, nobody worked for Uber, Snapchat, Etsy, or Pinterest. No one worked in the "App Economy" making games like Clash of Clans or Candy Crush because none of these even existed yet!

If people had always stuck in the mindset of what they wanted to be when they were younger, these companies would never have been created, nor would all of the cool jobs that came with them.

Instead of dwelling on your future career at this point, think about your career mindset. Are you someone who won't stop searching for a great career until you love Mondays? Or will you find satisfaction in settling for a job with a good income but no personal enjoyment?

One thing that college will offer you is the choice between the two and the flexibility to change your mind later.

**1. List three activities that you're good at or are meaningful to you.**

#1.

#2.

#3.

**2. List three things you aren't necessarily good at but think are important or "cool."**

#1.

#2.

#3.

**3. Choose three majors based on your responses to questions 1 and 2.** Don't be afraid to choose majors in crazy fields like Comic Art, Nautical Archaeology, or Theme Park Engineering!

Remember, you're the one who has to take the classes, so pick something that genuinely interests you.

#1.

#2.

#3.

**4.** Write three brief letters to yourself, each from your point of view as a 30-year-old who graduated with one of the majors you selected. Write about your reasons for choosing the major, what job you have now, what your daily life is like, what your biggest challenges are, and what your definition of success is in that field.

Letter #1

Major:

Letter #2

Major:

Letter #3

Major:

# Part F

# College Visits - A Journal

If you cannot visit the campus in person, go to https://campustours.com/

**College Name:**
**Date Visited:**
**Day of the Week:**

Initial Impressions:

    a. Were Students on Campus?

    b. If so, describe what they were doing (*e.g., walking to class, hanging out, eating lunch, playing frisbee on the grass, reading while scootering through traffic, crying about a midterm, etc.*)

    c. What were your first thoughts when you arrived on campus? (*Describe the atmosphere, the campus layout, and any specific details that stood out to you. What was your reaction to seeing the campus in person?*)

d. What did you do while on campus? What was your favorite thing to do there? What made it different than your high school campus?

e. How did the campus environment make you feel? (*Think about the energy, architecture, and overall vibe. Did you feel comfortable and welcomed? Explain why or why not?*)

f. Do you see yourself at this college? Why or why not?

g. What are your overall thoughts on applying to and eventually attending this college?

**College Name:**
**Date Visited:**
**Day of the Week:**

Initial Impressions:

    a. Were Students on Campus?

    b. If so, describe what they were doing (*e.g., walking to class, hanging out, eating lunch, playing frisbee on the grass, reading while scootering through traffic, crying about a midterm, etc.*)

    c. What were your first thoughts when you arrived on campus? (*Describe the atmosphere, the campus layout, and any specific details that stood out to you. What was your reaction to seeing the campus in person?*)

d. What did you do while on campus? What was your favorite thing to do there? What made it different than your high school campus?

e. How did the campus environment make you feel? (*Think about the energy, architecture, and overall vibe. Did you feel comfortable and welcomed? Explain why or why not?*)

f. Do you see yourself at this college? Why or why not?

g. What are your overall thoughts on applying to and eventually attending this college?

**College Name:**
**Date Visited:**
**Day of the Week:**

Initial Impressions:

    a. Were Students on Campus?

    b. If so, describe what they were doing (*e.g., walking to class, hanging out, eating lunch, playing frisbee on the grass, reading while scootering through traffic, crying about a midterm, etc.*)

    c. What were your first thoughts when you arrived on campus? (*Describe the atmosphere, the campus layout, and any specific details that stood out to you. What was your reaction to seeing the campus in person?*)

d. What did you do while on campus? What was your favorite thing to do there? What made it different than your high school campus?




e. How did the campus environment make you feel? (*Think about the energy, architecture, and overall vibe. Did you feel comfortable and welcomed? Explain why or why not?*)

f. Do you see yourself at this college? Why or why not?

g. What are your overall thoughts on applying to and eventually attending this college?

# Part G
# The College Experience - An Interview

This is an optional assignment for you to learn more about college by asking current college students important questions about their experience. Sample questions for them are below:

1. What university do you go to, and what does your typical day look like?

2. What has surprised you (both inside and outside the classroom) the most in college so far?

3. How have your classes been? What's your favorite? What's your most challenging?

4. Are you currently working? If so, how have you balanced your work and school responsibilities?

5. How is your social life? How are you meeting new people?

6. What resources on campus have been most helpful to you?

7. If you could go back in time and speak with your high school self, what would your advice be?

Any additional questions/thoughts:

# Part H

# The Career Experience - An Interview

This is an optional assignment for you to learn more about careers by asking current adults important questions about their experience. Sample questions for them are below:

1. What is your career, and what does a typical day look like?

2. What has surprised you the most about your career so far?

3. What is your favorite part of your job?

4. What is the worst part of your job?

5. What is your relationship like with your colleagues? Do you work together often?

6. Where do you see yourself in 5 years?

7. If you could go back in time and speak with your high school self, what would your advice be?

Any additional questions/thoughts:

# Part I

# My Own Experience - An Interview

1. What experiences have shaped my life?

2. What are my greatest strengths? How do I display these strengths? And how often?

3. What am I proud of?

4. What do I need/want to work on?

5. Which of my strengths do I want to continue to develop and use in my career as an adult?

6. What types of jobs do I think I'd enjoy the least? Why?

7. What do I value most in life?

8. How will my career be aligned with my values?

# Part J

# Avoiding For-Profit Colleges

All the schools we've discussed in this book have been non-profit universities, and that's for a good reason. This section provides a quick look into for-profit universities, a popular college choice, especially for many working adults who decide to go back to school.

These universities seem like an easy path to success due to their easy application requirements and near-guaranteed admission policies. Why do you think they made the application and admission policy extremely easy? To learn more about any school, **look at the facts related to how students experience the school.**

We can find individual stories of success and failure at any university, but how are students doing overall?

1. One of the most popular for-profit schools, the University of Phoenix - Arizona, saw just 2% of its students who started in 2017-2018 graduate (within 4 years).

# 2%!

That means out of 100 students, 98 paid and didn't receive a degree within the expected time. No. Don't listen to those who try to justify this graduation rate. This has been going on for decades.

2. Many of their students end up in financial distress. Students at the University of Phoenix - Arizona had a loan default rate of 13.5% in 2012, bringing it down to 8.7% in 2018. This amounted to THOUSANDS of students who could not repay what they borrowed to attend. (The most recent data (2020) is skewed because of the loan deferment allowed during COVID...)

3. The practices exposed at another common non-profit College, ITT Tech, led to its closing. The story of ITT Tech's rise and fall is just another example of how for-profit schools tend to take advantage of their students, doing whatever they can to make a profit.[53]

Despite these shortcomings, some people view for-profit universities as a good solution due to their relatively low tuition rates and flexible application deadlines and requirements.

Can you think of reasons a university would admit nearly every applicant with a high school diploma and keep tuition prices under $20,000?

Does this strategy provide more benefits for the corporation than for its students?

Would you prefer to attend a university that focuses on providing an education to as many people as possible or one that strives to provide the highest quality education possible?

**When it comes to for-profit universities, just say _____.**

---

[53] http://gizmodo.com/how-itt-tech-screwed-students-and-made-millions-1786654315

# Part K

# Starting Points for Transfer Students

## Reasons for Choosing (or not) this Pathway

I often hear students' desire to take the pathway of community college → transfer → 4-year university. Sometimes it has to do with saving money on "GEs" (General Education Courses). Sometimes, it has to do with getting better grades in community college (compared to high school) to gain admission to a more competitive 4-year university than those that offered them admission straight out of high school.

Both are valid reasons for going to community college with plans to transfer. With that said, it is important to consider a few things:

1. A first-year experience at a 4-year university teaches you more than solely what you learn in the classroom. Some folks see value in the independence, community resources, dorm life, etc., that you find at 4-year universities – and that value could be worth the additional cost per unit of your general education classes.

2. You may have the opportunity to take a general education class at a 4-year university that actually inspires you and your future education and career path. Instead of taking a GE to simply "get it out of the way," you may find the education itself is worth the additional cost...

3. Transferring is work (psychological and physical)—don't expect it to be easy or automatic—if it were, transfer rates would be much higher!

## Key Points to Success

1. Check the transfer requirements (online and with an advisor) for the four-year universities you want to transfer to.

- Taking Classic Rock of the 60s at your community college? Cool course, but it might not count for anything when you're trying to transfer to a 4-year university.

2. Register for classes when it's your time!!

- Make sure you get the classes you need with the professors you want! Pretend you're buying concert tickets that will be sold out soon after they go on sale. Set a reminder and get on your computer when it's your time. When it comes time to register, procrastination is an enemy.

3. If available, apply for a transfer program to guarantee your admission to the 4-year you're looking to transfer to!

- In California, it's called "TAG" or "TSP." In Virginia, it's called "GAA." In Maryland, it's called "MTAP." Ask your counselor or do more research on your state to see how you can guarantee your admission to a 4-year university (if your desired 4-year participates in such a program).

4. Make a plan and keep at it!

- After high school, you need to be proactive. You will be one student out of thousands at your local community college. You'll need to take on more responsibility for scheduling your classes and sticking to your plan.

- Schedule meetings with an advisor to get expert feedback and advice. They won't know you need help unless you ask! Prepare a list of questions ahead of time. These questions might include:

  - Am I on track to transfer to University XYZ, beginning Fall/Spring Semester of 20XX?

  - If I am considering changing my major, which general education courses should I take here at the Community College to give me the best chance to graduate from University XYZ on time?

- Plan out your course schedule for your entire 2-year journey ahead of time.

- Re-evaluate your plan and your progress every semester.

- Study and stay focused on your goal. You can do it!!

5. Be careful balancing your work commitment with your school commitment. Research has suggested that students who work *less than* 20 hours per week have more time to study and work on assignments, lower stress levels, and better attention spans in class compared to peers who work more than 20 hours

per week.[54]

When you're in college, you're giving up your current income to receive greater income in the future.

## My Transfer Plans

**Community College I'll attend:**

**Length of time I'll be there:**

### Here are Two 4-year Universities I'm Considering

| University: | University: |
|---|---|
| **Requirements to transfer** | **Requirements to transfer** |
| | |

[54] Dundes, L., & Marx, J. (2006). Balancing work and academics in college: Why do students working 10 to 19 hours per week excel? *College Student Journal, 40*(4), 927-934.

**My Main Education Goal:**

**Dates I'm setting reminders to re-evaluate my plan and my progress toward my education goals:**

**Habits needed to transfer successfully:**

**People to hold me accountable:**

# Part L

# Starting Points for Students Starting at 4-year Universities

### Reasons for Choosing (or not) this Pathway

Independence, academic opportunities, community building, and access to resources—all might be reasons one chooses to go directly to a four-year university after high school.

If you live in a dorm on campus, you immediately become immersed in a community of other first-year students from diverse backgrounds, but with similar aspirations.

Adjusting to your university environment early and settling in for the long term may also help as you progress toward your degree. There will be fewer transitions once you move to a 4-year, and you can focus solely on your academics instead of also considering moving to a new school/location/community in another two years. You may also be more prepared to study abroad or change your major if and when desired.

You will get to know the resources available to you on and off campus. With less concern about where/how/when you'll transfer, you will likely have more time and opportunities to focus on summer internships and future career paths.

### Key Points to Success

1. Check the graduation requirements (online and with an advisor) for the major you're working toward.

2. Register for classes when it's your time!!

3. Connect with Professors and Advisors! These folks can provide great insight and support. Don't wait until you're struggling to start forming these relationships!

4. Some students go a little wild with their first taste of independence. This can

lead to academic probation or dropping out. Maintain a healthy academic/social/personal balance. No one will be nagging you to go to class each day, to study, or to get some rest on a Tuesday night. Make sure you take care of yourself and your responsibilities and surround yourself with others who do the same.

5. Starting at a 4-year university is a marathon, not a sprint. Stay focused on your goals, use available resources on and off campus, and believe in yourself. College is challenging because it's challenging content! You've got this!

6. Many jobs don't care much about your college G.P.A. – just that you graduate. A famous old saying is, "Cs get degrees." However, many high-demand (and high-paying) jobs will typically only interview students with a college G.P.A. above a certain threshold. Make sure you're aware of this as you go through college!

## My University Plans

**University I'll attend:**

**Length of time I'll be there:**

**The major I'll be studying:**

**The minor I'll be studying (if applicable):**

**I am interested in studying abroad:  Yes / No / Unsure**

**I am interested in summer internships: Yes/ No / Unsure**

**My Main Education Goal:**

**Dates I'm setting reminders to re-evaluate my plan and my progress toward my education goals:**

**Habits needed to earn my degree on time:**

**People to hold me accountable:**

# Part M

# Starting Points for Undocumented Students

## THE UNFRIENDLIES

I'm not going to go over the specific laws of every state, but you should know that three states - Alabama, South Carolina, and Georgia - have either directly or indirectly disallowed Dreamers from attending their public colleges. There are a few more states that require Dreamers to pay higher non-resident tuition for their public colleges, even if they've lived there for many years.[55]

## THE FRIENDLIES

As of 2024, 25 states allow Dreamers to receive in-state tuition rates.[2] Qualifying for in-state tuition will save you thousands of dollars every year. Of the 25 providing in-state tuition rates, 19 and Washington D.C. provide access to additional financial aid from the state itself.

Here is a list of useful resources for undocumented students by state: https://www.higheredimmigrationportal.org/states/

## THE LAW TO PROTECT YOU AND YOUR PARENTS

If you or your parents are worried about being reported to ICE, please know that there's a law called the **Family Educational Rights and Privacy Act (FERPA)** that protects the privacy of your records at all K-12 schools, as well as public and private colleges and universities. Basically, this means they can't tell others about your immigration status.

The U.S. Department of Education also released a guide to support Dreamers, clarifying their legal rights and providing the necessary steps to take on their journey to college.

Check it out here:

http://www2.ed.gov/about/overview/focus/supporting-undocumented-youth.pdf

---

[55] https://www.higheredimmigrationportal.org/states/

Most importantly, **do not enter false information on your college applications**—this could result in your admission being revoked.

## QUICK TIPS: COLLEGE APPLICATIONS

The following tips are for Dreamers applying to UCs.[4] Keep in mind: this is one example. Applications to other schools will likely look different, so be sure to research application instructions and tips for other schools you're interested in.

1.     Whenever it is required, leave your Social Security Number (SSN) information blank. DO NOT put in a fake number - this will only cause you headaches later on. If you still have a DACA SSN or ITIN (Individual Tax Payer Identification Number), you should input that.

2.     For "Country of Citizenship," you should choose "No Selection" to avoid being asked further about your residency status.

3.     Some information they'll ask for, like "Parent Citizenship Status," won't affect your admission decision (it's just for informational purposes), but if you're not comfortable answering, just leave it blank.

To see all of the steps for applying to a UC as a Dreamer, go here:

https://admission.universityofcalifornia.edu/tuition-financial-aid/types-of-aid/who-can-get-financial-aid/ca-dream-act.html

## CALIFORNIA DREAMIN'

Now you know there's support out there for you to apply and gain admission to college, but what about paying for it?

The answer is in the **California Dream Act:** your gateway to receive in-state tuition and qualify for financial aid from the state of California and your university. If you don't live in California, use Google to see if your state has its own version of the Dream Act - some have it, others don't.

You qualify for the California Dream Act if you don't have a social security number and meet the following criteria:[5]

1. You've attended high school in California for at least three years.

2. You'll graduate from a California high school or pass the CHSPE or GED.

3. You're going to go to college in California.

4. If it applies to you, you'll complete an affidavit to legalize your immigration status once you're eligible.

At first, these were the criteria for giving students something called AB 540 status. But they're also the criteria to qualify for two new laws that were passed, making up the California Dream Act. Here are the details about this set of helpful laws:

1. **AB 540** - this bill was signed in 2001 before the CA Dream Act existed. It allows Dreamers to qualify for in-state tuition as long as they meet the criteria listed above.

2. **AB 130** - this bill, signed into law in 2011, allows Dreamers to apply for and receive scholarships (not from the state government) to attend public colleges.

3. **AB 131** - this bill, also signed into law in 2011, allows Dreamers to apply for and receive financial aid from the state of California.

The California Dream Act doesn't technically give you California residency, but it does give you similar rights and opportunities as California residents.

If you're eligible for AB 540 status, you should *not* fill out the FAFSA. Instead, you should complete the **CA Dream Act Application** and something called the **Non-SSN GPA form**.

Also, if you're applying to a private university, be sure to check with them to see if you need to complete the CSS Profile.

After submitting the Dream Act Application and Non-SSN GPA form, you may qualify for one or more of the following financial aid opportunities:

- Cal Grants

- High School Entitlement Cal Grant A & B

- CCC Transfer Entitlement Cal Grant A & B

- Cal Grant C

- Grants from the Cal State schools and the UC system (like the UC

Blue and Gold Opportunity Plan!)

- Chafee Grant (if you've been in foster care at some point)

- Middle-Class Scholarship (if your family income is less than $150,000 per year)

- "EOP" The Educational Opportunity Program (additional advising, tutoring, and other support for low-income students)

- Some university and private scholarships (like the $33,000 **thedream.us** scholarship for those who are eligible for both AB540 status and DACA)

Remember, these are all grants and scholarships, so *you don't have to pay them back!*

## CALIFORNIA DREAM LOAN PROGRAM

Starting in 2016, Dreamers attending four-year public universities in California (UCs or CSUs) can receive another form of financial aid: student loans.

As I mentioned in Chapter 6, the bad news about student loans is that students *do have to repay the money* they receive, plus interest.

The good news about the CA DREAM Loan Program is that interest rates are *fixed* and *the same rate* as Federal Direct Subsidized Loans, and just like those subsidized federal loans, you won't be charged interest while you're in school at least half-time.

Remember, if you're offered a loan in your financial aid package, only accept it if you truly need it.

## AB 540 FINANCIAL AID SUMMARY

| AB 540 Students Qualify For: | AB 540 Students Don't Qualify For: |
| --- | --- |
| In-state tuition (at UCs, CSUs, and California Community Colleges. | Federal Grants |

| AB 540 Students Qualify For: | AB 540 Students Don't Qualify For: |
| --- | --- |
| UC Grants | Federal Loans |
| CSU Grants | Federal Work-Study |
| Cal Grants | |
| Private Scholarships | |
| EOP | |
| DREAM Loans | |

## THE DEADLINE

The CA Dream Act Application becomes available on October 1 and is due **March 2** each year. Just do it in October so you don't forget or find yourself scrambling before the deadline. To receive Cal Grants, you must submit your school-certified Non-SSN GPA form by the same deadline.

## DREAM ACT APPLICATION TIPS

Things change! Make sure you verify that the tips below are up-to-date and reflect what you should do!!

- The Dream Act does not ask for your Social Security Number (SSN); if your parents have SSNs, enter them into the application. Enter all zeros if your parents do not have SSNs or other Tax ID Numbers.

- If you're a male between 18 and 25, you must register for the Selective Service to receive state financial aid. You can register at a post office—no social security number is required.

- If your parents still need to file their taxes (you're asked to provide tax info during the application process), have them estimate their income and taxes for last year. If your parents do not make enough money to file taxes, mark "Will Not File" on your application.

- Your taxes help prove whether or not you need financial aid, so you should encourage your parents to file their taxes using an ITIN (if they are undocumented). It's important that your parents feel safe filing taxes. Have them talk to others who can ease their concerns about their privacy, and let them know that the IRS (the organization that collects taxes and tax info) has confidentiality rules that protect your parents against immigration enforcement.

- When you make changes, your parents must re-sign your application using their electronic PIN.

# Part N

# Your Calendar

This calendar is here to help you plan key reminders about college and financial aid. Fill in the blanks and write notes to personalize it based on your goals throughout your senior year!

## AUGUST

|  | During the Week | On the Weekend |
|---|---|---|
| **Week 1** | | |
| **Week 2** | | |
| **Week 3** | | |
| **Week 4** | | |

**Big Goals**

# SEPTEMBER

| | During the Week | On the Weekend |
|---|---|---|
| Week 1 | | |
| Week 2 | | |
| Week 3 | | |
| Week 4 | | |

Big Goals

# OCTOBER

| | During the Week | On the Weekend |
|---|---|---|
| **Week 1** | | |
| **Week 2** | | |
| **Week 3** | | |
| **Week 4** | | |

Big Goals

# NOVEMBER

| | During the Week | On the Weekend |
|---|---|---|
| **Week 1** | | |
| **Week 2** | | |
| **Week 3** | | |
| **Week 4** | | |

**Big Goals**

# DECEMBER

|  | During the Week | On the Weekend |
|---|---|---|
| Week 1 | | |
| Week 2 | | |
| Week 3 | | |
| Week 4 | | |

Big Goals

# JANUARY

| | During the Week | On the Weekend |
|---|---|---|
| Week 1 | | |
| Week 2 | | |
| Week 3 | | |
| Week 4 | | |

**Big Goals**

# FEBRUARY

|  | During the Week | On the Weekend |
|---|---|---|
| Week 1 | | |
| Week 2 | | |
| Week 3 | | |
| Week 4 | | |

Big Goals

# MARCH

|  | During the Week | On the Weekend |
|---|---|---|
| Week 1 | | |
| Week 2 | | |
| Week 3 | | |
| Week 4 | | |

**Big Goals**

# APRIL

|  | During the Week | On the Weekend |
|---|---|---|
| **Week 1** | | |
| **Week 2** | | |
| **Week 3** | | |
| **Week 4** | | |

**Big Goals**

# MAY

| | During the Week | On the Weekend |
|---|---|---|
| **Week 1** | | |
| **Week 2** | | |
| **Week 3** | | |
| **Week 4** | | |

**Big Goals**

# JUNE

| | During the Week | On the Weekend |
|---|---|---|
| **Week 1** | | |
| **Week 2** | | |
| **Week 3** | | |
| **Week 4** | | |

Big Goals

# JULY

| | During the Week | On the Weekend |
|---|---|---|
| Week 1 | | |
| Week 2 | | |
| Week 3 | | |
| Week 4 | | |

**Big Goals**

# Part 0

# About the Author

My experience is likely different from the one you're looking for, but that's the great thing about college—there are so many ways to make it your own.

I'm not here to tell you how to live your life in college; I'm just trying to show you how to make this incredible opportunity a reality.

I completed four years of college. I lived both on-campus and off-campus, took classes in person and online, switched majors, joined a fraternity, and worked on campus as a work-study student at the Los Angeles Caregiver Resource Center.

I experienced the stress of back-to-back final exams and the concern for family members I had left back at home. I loved the craziness of dorm life, meeting great friends from around the country and around the world, and rooting on our football team as they competed for a national championship. I spent my summers doing everything from working at a local bagel shop to interning at a hedge fund services firm in Dublin, Ireland. I earned most of my credits at USC, but the summer after I switched majors I took a class at a local community college so I could catch up on coursework and graduate on time.

In high school, people raised eyebrows when they heard I wanted to attend an "expensive" private university like USC. Considering that my mom supported my three siblings and me on a teacher's salary, I had plenty of excuses to listen to the critics who doubted I could make it work. There were paths of less resistance right in front of my face.

But USC became affordable with grants, scholarships, and work-study. I learned that sometimes the colleges with the most money provide the most financial aid. The financial aid I received to attend USC opened the door for opportunities to better understand myself and the world, make lifelong friendships, and have a career in a field I love.

## Finance

After graduating from USC in 2007 with a business degree, I worked in private wealth management for a large Swiss bank (UBS) in Los Angeles and Beverly Hills. I learned how to make personalized financial plans and to help others analyze and acheive their financial goals. It's not a coincidence that this book discusses similar ideas.

Despite enjoying finance, I came to realize that I wasn't living out my true purpose in life. The salary was good, the stock market was interesting, but I was drawn to helping where I was needed more.

## Teaching

After a few years working a 9-to-5 job, I arrived at a turning point: Either I go on an adventure and look deeper into the meaning of my life, or I watch time slowly pass by and find temporary comfort in the status from my banking job and the things I could buy. I looked to my faith and my family. I felt strongly that:

> It is the heart that makes a man rich. He is rich according to what he is, not according to what he has. - *Henry Ward Beecher*

I found three enticing opportunities that could help me find what I was looking for – crushing grapes in New Zealand (wwoof.net), DJing in Alaska (knom.org), and teaching in Micronesia (worldteach.org). After my application to WorldTeach was accepted, I decided to take the risk and leave my job. In the following three months, I said goodbye to my coworkers, sold my BMW, gave my iPhone to my sister, and boarded a plane to Kosrae, Micronesia. Suddenly I was 5,000 miles away from home on a tiny island in the middle of the Pacific Ocean.

During my year teaching math and English in Kosrae, I discovered that helping young people succeed was more important than anything else I had done so far in my life. I found newfound excitement in everyday life. When I returned to California, I went to graduate school and earned my teaching credential and a master's degree in Digital Teaching and Learning at Azusa Pacific University.

Since then, I've been teaching math and finance in public and charter schools. I've continued striving to grow as an educator through professional development, working with the Wharton School of Business at UPenn's San Francisco campus, and as a Hollyhock Fellow at Stanford University.

## MY REASONS FOR WRITING THIS BOOK

I'm a high school teacher who's passionate about helping students become financially responsible, self-aware adults. Every student should have access to the financial aid resources that are out there. Each year I work with students who are discouraged by the high cost of college. It's unacceptable that most students never have the opportunity to do proper research into the costs and benefits of all their options within higher education.

In most high schools, you're expected to make an extremely stressful decision involving tens of thousands of dollars without even knowing what "net price" means!

If I asked you to take a test with consequences that could affect the rest of your life without teaching you the material, that would sound pretty crazy, right? Unfortunately, this is the situation many high school students find themselves in when it comes to paying for college.

I wrote this book to show you how, through the power of financial aid, your college costs can drop dramatically—in some cases, to $0—at many amazing colleges!

I want you to feel confident making *your own* decisions about college. After all, you're the one who will live with the consequences.

# Part P

# Extra Space Just For You...

Blank 1

Blank 2

Blank 3

Blank 4

Blank 5

Blank 6

Blank 7

Blank 8

Blank 9

Blank 10

Lined 1

Lined 2

Lined 3

Lined 4

187

Lined 5

Lined 6

Lined 8

Lined 9

Lined 10

Made in United States
Troutdale, OR
12/20/2024

27021602R00111